IN THE
NATIONAL INTEREST

General Sir John Monash once exhorted a graduating class to 'equip yourself for life, not solely for your own benefit but for the benefit of the whole community'. At the university established in his name, we repeat this statement to our own graduating classes, to acknowledge how important it is that common or public good flows from education.

Universities spread and build on the knowledge they acquire through scholarship in many ways, well beyond the transmission of this learning through education. It is a necessary part of a university's role to debate its findings, not only with other researchers and scholars, but also with the broader community in which it resides.

Publishing for the benefit of society is an important part of a university's commitment to free intellectual inquiry. A university provides civil space for such inquiry by its scholars, as well as for investigations by public intellectuals and expert practitioners.

This series, In the National Interest, embodies Monash University's mission to extend knowledge and encourage informed debate about matters of great significance to Australia's future.

Professor Margaret Gardner AC
President and Vice-Chancellor,
Monash University

JO DYER
BURNING DOWN THE HOUSE: RECONSTRUCTING MODERN POLITICS

MONASH
UNIVERSITY
PUBLISHING

Burning Down the House: Reconstructing Modern Politics
© Copyright 2022 Jo Dyer

Monash University Publishing
Matheson Library Annexe
40 Exhibition Walk
Monash University
Clayton, Victoria 3800, Australia
https://publishing.monash.edu

Monash University Publishing brings to the world publications which advance the best traditions of humane and enlightened thought.

ISBN: 9781922633002 (paperback)
ISBN: 9781922633026 (ebook)

Series: In the National Interest
Editor: Louise Adler
Project manager & copyeditor: Paul Smitz
Designer: Peter Long
Typesetter: Cannon Typesetting
Proofreader: Gillian Armitage

Printed in Australia by Ligare Book Printers

A catalogue record for this book is available from the National Library of Australia.

For Kate, whose courage inspires mine.

BURNING DOWN THE HOUSE: RECONSTRUCTING MODERN POLITICS

Kakistocracy—a state or society led by its least suitable or competent citizens. Welcome to Australia, 2021.

After the numbing surrealness of the last two pandemic-inflected years, it's easy to forget there was a time before the deadening mediocrity of our current political system and the leaders it has coughed up. Now, accustomed as we are to relentless disappointments and embarrassments and shocking cruelties, the notion that we can do things differently, better, expansively, with ambition, generosity, camaraderie, is alien. And that's understandable. The pivotal moments in online time-wasting across the lockdowns may have been diverting—Sarah Cooper's lip-syncing! Ted Lasso! Sally McManus's hair!—but the standout moments in the political arena across 2020–21 that seemed to ricochet through the subsequent weeks and months, and, heavy with resonance, led us to where we are now, have not been uplifting. As we edge into a new normal, we seem an exhausted, cynical nation. We yearn for something bigger, better, but, dispirited by fires, and COVID, and the state-against-state dystopia we've lived through, we are caught in a tragic downward spiral of poor leadership and sullen politics.

This essay surveys those moments of the last two years that demonstrate how hopelessly we have lost our way, how thoroughly we have been compromised. It looks at the failure of leadership that has brought us to this moment in time, and questions whether our alleged two-party system can break our dangerous cycle.

It posits that we risk becoming inured to the plummeting standards of our public life, mere bystanders before the procession of the tawdry, terrible choices made by our government, from Black Summer to now, normalising their misjudgements, cruelty and deflections with our careless inattention or lazy apathy. Perhaps we're reassured because those against whom we often judge ourselves—the Forever Friends of the newly minted, already tarnished AUKUS committee—are wrestling with their own political crises, the United Kingdom in denial they dealt themselves the Joker, the United States burdened with the legacy of a Trump that took no tricks. As truth and integrity fall victim to the government's rougher-than-usual handling, we must guard against not just entrenching vapid politics over policy, but the government's disdain for policy altogether.

Finally, some hope. Perhaps it is true that despair comes before the dawn, but regardless, around the nation people are awakening to the idea that we are devastatingly ill-served by a venal, tribal government unwilling or unable to change, and contemptuous of those it is elected to serve. People for whom politics has been background noise, or an occasionally entertaining diversion, are recognising that if things are to change, someone has to step up and change them.

'If not us, then who?' asks independent candidate for Goldstein Zoe Daniel, echoing Hillel the Elder. Tired of wallowing in disgust and frustration, more people are now prepared to step forward and be part of the change. Perhaps we had to plumb the depths for this energy to be unleashed but, oh, what depths we have plumbed, and oh, what pain has been caused.

THE SKY IS BURNING

As 2019 drew to a close, an innocent pre-COVID time, Australia was engulfed in the crisis of a bushfire season that was one of the worst we had known. Those living through the Black Summer endured experiences ranging from having to stay inside to breathe normally, to fleeing in advance of fires so intense they developed their own weather systems. Lives were lost, boundless species were wiped out, and Australians were confronted by apocalyptic imagery of people huddled in terror on beaches cast with an eerie orange hue, looking back at blazing homes and landscapes. Some rowed desperately out to sea in small boats to escape the flames, the masks covering their faces an odd presage of the many months to come.

Those watching in horror from afar passed around Ross Garnaut's quote from his 2008 report on climate change that described Australia's looming fate, project-ing that 'fire seasons will start earlier, end slightly later, and generally be more intense ... This effect increases over time, but should be directly observable by 2020.'[1] And so it was. We all observed directly what Garnaut had foretold. In the baking heat and dry air, we shivered at his prescience and considered what it was most of us had lived through but thirty-three had not, what it meant that the worst-case scenarios were coming true.

At the height of the infernos, Prime Minister Scott Morrison took a holiday at a beachside resort in Hawaii and his office lied about it. It was not until photos turned up online of the Prime Minister posing goofily in Honolulu alongside disbelieving Australian tourists that his staff 'fessed up. Morrison later blamed his children for his decision to go overseas and said it was fine anyway because he didn't hold a hose. There would have been no hoses to spare in any case because Morrison's government had failed to make funds available for the urgent firefight-ing equipment requested by a delegation of twenty-three former fire and emergency leaders with whom he refused to meet. Peeved at the truncation of, and fallout from, his international jaunt, Morrison charged up to devastated towns laid waste by the fire and pumped the reluctant hands of reeling residents while secretly laying on his own. He announced bushfire emergency relief funds that would later be spent in marginal seats in North Queensland.[2]

As the fires terrorised the continent's eastern and southern coasts, it was not, we were breathlessly told, the time to discuss climate change. That would be a gauche politicisation of a tragedy while people and their homes remained at risk. As ash showered city streets far from the fire's theatre, however, it was acceptable for government ministers to lecture us in an entirely apolitical way about how the fires weren't caused by climate change because back-burning could have saved us. National MPs were all accusatory stares and arched eyebrows as they took to the governmental bully pulpit at both the state and national levels to lament the refusal of the Greens and Labor, who held power in neither, to allow more hazard-reduction fires. This, and the disempowerment of landowners by state regulations, they said, was to blame for the cata-strophic fires. Oh, and the hordes of arsonists they asserted were deliberately wreaking havoc. The valiant efforts of police and firefighters to refute the existence of an arson army did not get the same traction from the media outlets that so reliably boosted the government's false narratives.

Many drew links between the Australian Government's stonewalling of discussions about climate change while the country burned, with America's insistence that the time to debate gun control was definitely not in the heart-stopping aftermath of another mass fatality that had seen little chil-dren and their teachers slaughtered in their classrooms, or the devout shot as they prayed, or concertgoers and clubbers picked off as they danced. We knew of the gov-ernment's wanton attitude to climate change, but their obduracy in the face of the Black Summer tragedy and the calamity of Australia's relentlessly worsening conditions was still difficult to behold. Not only do they not believe in climate change—the weather's been fluctuating forever, *the Global Energy Sector*, is clear: beyond the projects already committed to as of 2021, there can be no new oil or gas fields approved for development if we are to get to net zero by 2050. Neither can there be new coalmines or mine extensions, and coal-fuelled power stations should be phased out of developed countries by 2030. Described as 'the world's first comprehensive study of how to transition to a net zero energy system by 2050 while ensuring stable and affordable energy supplies, providing universal energy access, and enabling robust economic growth',[3] the report also makes it clear that no new fossil fuel projects are required if we get the rest of the policy settings right. 'The road to Net Zero is narrow,' it reads. 'Staying on it requires the massive deployment of all available clean energy technologies.'[4] Despite its rhetorical commitment to net zero by 2050, Australia seems further away from this than ever. What is behind our refusal to behave rationally in the face of an imminent threat?

'State capture' is another term that disseminated more widely across 2020–21. In his book *Full Circle*, Scott Ludlum describes being in Kenya and sitting in on a meeting with Kenya Tuitakayo, an emerging network of social movements demanding 'the Kenya we want'. Their charter reads:

> The Kenyan state and public finance are under capture by a small but powerful group of individuals, who have directed public planning and development towards their own primitive greed and accumulation to the detriment of everyone else.

'Without exaggeration,' Ludlum writes, 'you could substitute the word "Kenya" for "Australia" and the sentence still lands.'[5]

Australia is being held hostage by a group of politicians, business leaders and their useful climate sceptics. Marian Wilkinson documents their efforts in her book *The Carbon Club*, describing the highly coordinated, well-funded campaign to resist effective action on climate change specifically by undermining the science that underpins it. This campaign has been underway since the formation of the Global Climate Coalition in the lead-up to the UN Earth Summit in Rio de Janeiro in 1992. With a membership that includes the world's largest fossil fuel producers, the Global Climate Coalition continues its ferocious backlash to this day, and Australia's climate policy has been mired in it from the start. Since Rio, Australian governments of both political persuasions have capitulated to the Carbon Club and pursued the rigid rule of 'No Regrets'. 'Australia would only reduce its greenhouse gas emissions if it didn't cost us,' Wilkinson writes. 'There should be no net impact on the economy.'[6]

Many people were surprised to hear that a key recommendation of Scott Morrison's COVID-19 Commission Advisory Board in the early odd days of the pandemic was the construction of a gas pipeline across Australia, pondering its relevance to the health crisis at hand. But then we were reminded that commission chair Nev Power, hand-picked by Morrison, is on the board, and a major shareholder of, oil and gas exploration company Strike Energy, and suddenly it made more sense.

Mining executives, lobbyists and other fully paid-up members of the Carbon Club abound in the government's orbit. Morrison's office is populated by them. His chief of staff, John Kunkel, is the former deputy CEO of the Minerals Council of Australia (MCA), the organisation that thoughtfully provided a now infamous lump of coal for Morrison to brandish in parliament, carefully lacquered to keep in the dust habitually smeared on Coalition faces before fronting cameras. The former CEO of the MCA, Brendan Pearson, also served in Morrison's office as an industry and trade adviser before securing the role of ambassador to the Organisation for Economic Co-operation and Development and heading to Paris to be reunited with another former boss, Mathias Cormann. Others in the Prime Minister's Office, such as Yaron Finkelstein and Stephanie Wawn, are long-term lobbyists for the mining industry via companies including Crosby Textor and Capital Hill Advisory. Still other Coalition luminaries have graduated from pro-mining lobbying companies or think tanks directly into parliament—James McGrath, for example—or leadership roles in the organisational wing of the Liberal Party, such as its federal director, Andrew Hirst.

The close-knit relationships between senior members of the government and the fossil fuel industry are remarkable, the former moving seamlessly between being ministers or staffers, mining executives and directors, lobbyists and party donors, with money flowing effortlessly from our taxes in vast grants and subsidies to industry, and from industry back to the parties to help them retain government. They serve in each other's offices and on each other's boards and look out for each other's interests.[7] They are family.[8] Let us not forget that one of the most shameful moments in our recent history, the bugging of the government of Timor-Leste, was done by the Australian Secret Intelligence Service (ASIS) on our government's orders to advance the commercial interests of Woodside Petroleum. Key players in the authorisation of that illegal act, which even now the government tries to cover up with its punitive pursuit through the courts of lawyer Bernard Collaery, were later rewarded by Woodside. Ashton Calvert, secretary of the Department of Foreign Affairs and Trade (DFAT), of which ASIS is part, joined Woodside's board in 2005 after his retirement from the public service, and former foreign minister Alexander Downer took up a lucrative consulting job following his departure from parliament in 2008.

These cosy allies betray our friends and our future to bolster the tribe. The next generation is feeling betrayed too, and as the government sat on its hands with climate change, the kids got creative. In early 2021, eight high-school students, led by Anj Sharma, and with the assistance of the admirable 86-year-old Sister Brigid Arthur, previously best known for her advocacy work for refugees, brought a case against Environment Minister Sussan Ley. Ley was back from her stint on the backbench after being caught using her travel allowance to fly to the Gold Coast in a charter plane to boost her flying hours as a pilot, and to buy a holiday house while passing through—she'd also returned from her emergency trip to Europe to lobby United Nations Educational, Scientific and Cultural Organization delegates not to embarrass the government by listing the Great Barrier Reef as endangered, despite the fact it is endangered. The students argued the minister had a duty of care to consider the climate change impacts of approving the Vickery Extension open-cut coalmine project near the NSW town of Gunnedah. The minister, they suggested, should not make decisions that endangered the very planet on which they would have to try and live in the future. In finding for the plaintiffs, Bromberg J wrote:

> It is difficult to characterise in a single phrase the devastation that the plausible evidence presented in this proceeding forecasts for the Children. As Australian adults know their country, Australia will be lost and the World as we know it gone as well. The physical environment will be harsher, far more extreme and devastatingly brutal when angry. As for the human experience—quality of life, opportunities to partake in nature's treasures, the capacity to grow and prosper— all will be greatly diminished. Lives will be cut short. Trauma will be far more common and good health harder to hold and maintain. None of this will be the fault of nature itself. It will largely be inflicted by the inaction of this generation of adults, in what might fairly be described as the greatest inter-generational injustice ever inflicted by one generation of humans upon the next.[9]

Fighting words from Bromberg J! Weighing up evidence and making findings of fact are things we ask of our judges as part of their professional duties, and we accept they are qualified to do. In discharging his obligations, Bromberg J was emphatic in tone and language. His judgment was a creative and radical extension of well-established principles of tort law into climate change litigation. In finding the minister had a duty to the next generation not to damage them at some stage in the future with actions taken now, Bromberg J was breaking new legal ground. He said that by extending coalmines in this time of climate crisis, Ley—and by extension the government in which she served—would be causing harm to those to whom she owed a duty of care, harm that was unlawful and for which she would be held liable in the future (in a pyrrhic kind of way).

Bromberg J declined to grant a pre-emptive injunction to prevent the minister from taking the decision, believing she would not breach the duty of care once made aware that it had been found to exist by a decision of the court. He was wrong. Even as Ley announced she was going to appeal the court's decision, she went ahead and approved the mine extension. She approved two more shortly thereafter.[10] There are currently twenty new mines proposed in NSW alone,[11] and the government is pushing for the opening of at least five new 'strategic' gas basins.[12] Many of these will be provided subsidies, whether direct cash grants for R&D, like the $21 million handed over to Liberal Party donor Empire Energy's Beetaloo Basin fracking project, or tax concessions, or the establishment of expensive infrastructure. The entire remit of the Australian Rail Track Corporation, chaired by former Nationals leader Warren Truss, is to invest taxpayers' dollars in inland rail projects in order to transfer coal from mines to ports more efficiently; in the last two years, the corporation has been underwritten by us to the tune of around $700 million per annum. All up, the federal government provides $10.3 billion annually to subsidise fossil fuels, including $7.84 billion in fuel tax credits.[13]

All this when we know we have to phase out fossil fuel. The courts find so. The international community says so. The next generation demands so. That's what the 2021 United Nation's Climate Change Conference (COP26) was supposed to be about. We must wean ourselves off fossil fuel entirely and build a new economy that is not obsessed with burning and extracting, and, as the IEA makes clear, we already have the means to do so. Morrison, in his largely unattended speech at COP26, reached for rhetoric that he thought could excuse inaction. It is our scientists, technologists and entrepreneurs who will save us, he said, and we need to back them and their 'can-do capitalism'—as if it wasn't 'can-do-anything-we-like unchecked capitalism' that had brought us to this point, or that our scientists, technologists and entrepreneurs haven't already developed the solutions to our problems but are being ignored by a government that continues to support the fossil fuel industry.

We have joined the unholy alliance of Saudi Arabia, Russia, China, Brazil and India to stymie effective international action, not just as a laggard but as a spoiler.

The 'modelling' for the government's long-awaited net zero by 2050 'plan' relies heavily on offsets, the fantasy of carbon capture and storage, as yet unknown technology breakthroughs, and a laughable voluntary price on carbon that the government mostly pretends isn't there and can't explain why business would stump up for it anyway. It expands gas extractions by a third even as scientists insist that, as another fossil fuel, gas must be phased out in the same way as coal. Resources and Water Minister Keith Pitt proudly proclaims we will keep mining coal as long as there are people willing to buy it. Morrison says coal will be part of our economy for decades to come, and he did a jig on the approval of a new $18 billion gas project labelled by the Conservation Council of Western Australia as the most polluting fossil fuel development in recent memory.[14] The ink was barely dry on the pact we'd signed up to in Glasgow when Morrison's ministers advised us they had no intention of keeping the commitments they had voluntarily made.

PEOPLE LIKE US:
THE DESERVING UNEMPLOYED

Josh Frydenberg has described Monday 22 March 2020 as the worst day of his pandemic, a day that invoked the Great Depression.[15] Overnight, queues formed at Centrelink offices nationally, snaking down streets and around corners, as people responded to the forced closure of pubs, clubs and restaurants and the immediate loss of their jobs. Then government services minister

Stuart Robert was in charge of the Centrelink website, so naturally it crashed. For an excruciating moment, he tried to claim it was a denial-of-service attack before conceding Centrelink was simply not prepared for the massive influx of clients. Discomfited by the fact that 'ordinary people' were now joining the ranks of the unemployed in large numbers, the federal government doubled the JobSeeker allowance and removed draconian administrative 'mutual obligation' edicts for recipients that required them to apply for vast numbers of generally inappropriate jobs in order to show that they had. Thousands were lifted out of poverty at a keystroke—it was shown to be that simple. And yet it hadn't been done prior to the pandemic, and that March day Frydenberg found so confronting, for the many caught on the sharp end of poverty and living lives of gnawing insecurity. The anxious, exhausting existence of the apparently undeserving unemployed was entirely accepted, if not promoted; once the pandemic threatened the deserving unemployed, Frydenberg acted swiftly.

The JobSeeker initiative transformed people's lives. Welfare recipients described the blessed simple relief of not having to make choices between food and basic bills; of being able to buy a new pair of shoes for their children; of being able to invest in themselves a little, to relieve the constant painful itch of financial uncertainty. They were also freed from the more degrading and dehumanising aspects of dealing with Centrelink, a system riddled with punitive requirements of reporting, of participation in meaningless 'training' courses, of requiring immediate responses to intrusive questions, with failures to comply resulting in income being suspended for weeks at a time. Individual circumstances and commitments are rarely taken into account.

It took a pandemic for dignity to be restored. Temporarily. Why only temporarily? Because in less extreme times, the cruelty is the point. Ensuring that people have uncomfortable, difficult lives on welfare is necessary, we are told, to avoid them relaxing into laziness and bludging off the rest of us—'bludging' being that most loaded of terms describing that most reviled of behaviours by that most parasitic of rent seeker. Never mind that analysis of the expenditure patterns of the unemployed whose lives were transformed when they received the Coronavirus Supplement reveals that the money was spent wisely.

Andrew Charlton reported on Accenture analysis in an address to the National Press Club in November 2021: 'The largest amount, $85, was spent on household bills, electricity, phone, water; $70 of that extra money was spent on food; around $60 was spent on clothing and household goods; around $175 was saved or used to pay down debt.' Despite the evidence-free assertions from those advocating against an increase, when the JobSeeker beneficiaries received extra support, they spent it wisely, and quickly, in ways that stimulated our depressed economy. 'They didn't spend that money on frivolous or discretionary items,' said Charlton, and, crucially, 'They didn't withdraw from the labour market.' The evidence of the natural experiment enabled by the pandemic revealed that providing extra funds to JobSeeker recipients did not act as a disincentive to them to look for work. Instead, we learned that 'giving more money to lower income people has many positive benefits both to them and the community'.[16]

To date, the government has shown no inclination to apply the lessons learned from the pandemic. Instead of generosity, and in contrast to Morrison's expressed fervent desire to get government out of people's lives, it seeks to intrude further into the daily existence of welfare recipients, most notably through an expansion of the Indue card. Not only does the Indue card restrict what people receiving welfare benefits can buy and where they can buy it, thereby preventing users from seeking out cheaper prices at discount supermarkets or second-hand shops, the government pays a per-person annual fee to a private company for the privilege. While it is not a new phenomenon for the government to prefer to pay private companies exorbitant sums of money to do things that were previously within the remit of a valued public service, one does wonder why it is that the lives of the less fortunate can be measured so parsimoniously in welfare dollars, while taxpayer money can wash through our system seemingly endlessly to prop up fossil fuels, pay vast sums for consultants, and be committed to unnecessary infrastructure in marginal seats around election time. Governments make choices about money all the time. If they choose profit over people, and we choose them over others, we are complicit in these priorities.

Cruelty was also the point in the relentless pursuit of alleged welfare overpayments to the most vulnerable Australians, which became known as 'Robodebt'.

The illegal hounding of individuals who had received social welfare that an income-averaging algorithm decided, often erroneously, they were retrospectively not entitled to, was dreamed up by—who else?—Scott Morrison when social services minister, and it was a low point in recent Australian public policy. The onus of proof was reversed, so it was up to individuals to produce paperwork dating back up to seven years to demonstrate they didn't owe the debt the government asserted they did. In fact, the government continued to pursue the recovery policy for years after they'd been advised by their own departments it was illegal. At least five families believe Robodebt was a key contributor to the suicide of a loved one.

Why was the Robodebt money deemed so much more valuable by the government than the $29 billion wasted by the lazy drafting of the JobKeeper legislation, with its inexplicable failure to include a claw-back mechanism, even after the government was told that many companies were not experiencing the threshold 30 per cent decline in turnover that rendered them enduringly eligible for the cash? The government took no action to recover payments from the companies in question, nor from those that went on to increase their profits and who piped the JobKeeper windfall directly to executives via bonuses and to shareholders via dividends. This cavalier approach to mind-bogglingly large amounts of taxpayers' money made for a brutal contrast to the systemic persecution of the most vulnerable in our community.

The Administrative Appeals Tribunal (AAT) was to become the hero of the Robodebt saga, as it often does when called to reign in bureaucratic overreach. Judgments from its longest-serving member, Terry Carney, were made public in a Senate inquiry in February 2020. Carney had repeatedly warned that the government could not enforce the alleged welfare overpayments without proving the debt existed—he'd done so nearly three years before the Federal Court reached the same conclusion, bringing an end to the sorry saga. Despite his forty years of service, Carney's contract was not extended as a result, with the government replacing him and many other independent expert members with ex-Liberal parliamentarians, candidates and staffers.[17] The AAT's willingness to stand up to the government on such issues makes the wholesale stacking of the tribunal with the government's mates and fellow travellers even more worrying. Worse than the flagrancy with which they hand out well-paid positions to those unqualified to fill them, and treat quasi-judicial roles as sinecures to gift, is the potential neutering of a significant forum for justice.

There were other lessons we could have learned from the pandemic about surviving on low incomes. We could have acknowledged that precarious and casualised work is dangerous. Without access to sick leave, by necessity people will prioritise going to work to continue to earn money to feed themselves and their families rather than staying home to protect their health and that of the wider community. As it became clear which 'essential workers' really were essential, we could have reassessed the value we place on certain types of work, the people who do that work, and the remuneration we provide for it.

COMPASSION TAKES MANY FORMS

On 8 June 2021, a four-year-old girl was flown into Perth for emergency hospitalisation. She was suffering from pneumonia and septicaemia, medical conditions exacerbated if not caused by the difficult circumstances in which she'd been forcibly living for the past eighteen months. The little girl was Tharnicaa Murugappan, and she had contracted these illnesses while being held in detention on Christmas Island by the Australian Government after the Department of Home Affairs had enacted dawn raids on her home in the regional Queensland town of Biloela, ripping crying children from the arms of their screaming mother. Tharnicaa's family was bundled out of the modest bungalow they'd made their own in the five years since they'd settled in the community, dad Nadesalingam working at the local abattoir and volunteering at St Vinnies in his spare time, mum Priya focusing on their two small children.

So much about this sad story exemplifies the arbitrary cruelty of Australia's refugee policies of the last twenty years and the callous indifference we have shown to the impact deliberate political choices have had on innocent lives. Australia's obsession with refugees who arrive by boat is a result of careful political manipulation dating back to the Howard years. John Howard crafted a narrative of irresponsible queue jumpers that he then carefully wove into a dark tale of violent individuals willing to risk the lives of their children to secure visas in Australia via the 'children overboard' lie, then meshed this with the War on Terror. Even as we trumpeted the regimes they were fleeing as so heinous that we had to join American wars to topple them, we demonised the individuals who managed to get away. With overblown clash of civilisations–style rhetoric, Howard labelled them possible terrorists, exploiting the shock left in the wake of 9/11 to promote Western values as conflicting with and being endangered by the Muslim world, and recasting refugees to whom we owed legal protection under the *Migration Act* as an existential threat to our way of life.

The runaway success of this political strategy unleashed new enthusiasm for using refugees in a longer-term debased game. Australia began behaving in disturbing ways. We sent the Special Air Service to board the *Tampa* to repel desperate refugees and a horrified Norwegian sea captain. And then there is the dark story of *SIEV X*, a boat carrying 421 asylum seekers that went missing in October 2001 while we were monitoring it, then sank in international waters we were actively patrolling.

Early dishonest attempts by Howard and senior members of the military to shirk responsibility for the tragedy that resulted in the deaths of 146 children, 142 women and sixty-five men, by asserting the *SIEV X* sank in Indonesian waters, were comprehensively debunked at the Senate inquiry into the sinking. But sinister questions remain. What was the nature of the 'disruption program' regarding people-smuggling in Indonesia in which Australia was involved, and that was rumoured to include sabotaging boats? The director-general of Coastwatch, Rear Admiral Marcus Bonser, reported that, at the time, the area was 'being covered by what is probably the most comprehensive surveillance that I have seen in some 30 years of service'.[19] He testified to the inquiry that, despite (false) evidence that the Navy had received no information about the overloaded boat departing Indonesia for Christmas Island, the Navy had in fact received six detailed intelligence reports about *SIEV X* and its departure date from Indonesia, as well as its likely arrival on Christmas Island. Did Australia have knowledge of the boat's location at the point it foundered? Had we failed, wilfully or callously, to deliver assistance to people in grave need? Some of the forty-five survivors claimed two military-style vessels had approached those clinging desperately to detritus in the ocean, shone floodlights on the scene, then departed. Given this incident took place in the febrile environment of the 2001 Australian election campaign, it would have been inconvenient for the government if the survivors had been evacuated to our shores at this time. Indeed, within twenty-four hours of this heartbreaking calamity, then immigration minister Philip Ruddock said to the media that its potential deterrent effect meant 'This tragedy may have an upside'.[20]

Asylum seekers who did make it to those bits of Australia not excised from our migration zone during this period were dehumanised. Their faces were not depicted in any media. They were given numbers on arrival in the detention centres by which they were then called. Howard could not have been more thrilled when he hit on the idea of exploiting the poverty of our Pacific neighbours Papua New Guinea and Nauru by paying them vast sums of blood money to house our gulags. That way it was even easier to ensure that pesky journalists couldn't get too close to them—not least because Nauru gleefully increased the cost for them to even apply for a visa, from $200 to $8000; it also kept them far away from the jurisdiction of the Australian courts, which had an annoying habit of questioning the legality of some of the government's behaviour (even while endorsing the indefinite detention offshore). The camps themselves were run as militaristic prisons where people died from suicide, acts of murderous violence and criminal neglect. As immigration minister, Morrison became an enthusiastic withholder of information and humane treatment, behaviour which ultimately led to the government paying out millions to those it mistreated,[21] and those trying to help those it mistreated that the government went on to defame.[22]

The denial of desperately needed medical care observed in the case of Tharnicaa Murugappan in 2021 had an earlier fatal outing in the 2014 case of Hamid Kehazaei, a detainee on Manus Island whose severe illness was left without appropriate medical treatment despite his obvious suffering and repeated pleas for help. By the time he was finally flown to Brisbane for emergency care, he was brain dead. While in our care, Hamid died of an easily treatable condition that we had the capacity to treat but chose not to. When the country learned Tharnicaa was burning up from the same septicaemia, there was a sharp intake of breath from a suddenly terrified nation. Were we now in the process of killing a child? Past performance suggested it possible. Past performance suggested anything was possible.

With a developing backlash from a nation whose conscience flickered dimly at the sight of a terrified little girl, new home affairs minister Karen Andrews was interviewed on ABC Breakfast and asked if she'd show some compassion to the desperate family. With their two children born in Australia—something that formerly would have allowed automatic citizenship but which, following deft legislative work from Peter Dutton, now meant they were pejoratively known as 'anchor babies'—and with a community that loved them and continued to fight tenaciously for them, could they stay here? Andrews initially sought to hide behind the ongoing court proceedings necessitated by the earlier refusal of immigration ministers to exercise their discretion. Presenter Michael Rowland persisted, causing Andrews to finally respond, 'I am a very compassionate person by nature and I will never walk away from that. But compassion takes many different forms.'

It is unclear what dark forces Andrews thought were exhorting her to walk away from compassion. A further two questions were begged by her response. Exactly what form of compassion is it that requires the health of an imprisoned young girl to deteriorate to dangerous levels before her jailers deign to provide her with readily available medical care? And what kind of cognitive dissonance allows someone to indignantly assert they are a compassionate person while behaving in this manner?

LEAVE YOUR MATES BEHIND: THE FALL OF AFGHANISTAN

Australians like to think of themselves as good mates. John Howard even tried to get the word 'mateship' included in the preamble to our Constitution as one of the sacred tenets of our nation.[23] It was Howard, too, who in mid-2021 staged a last-minute intervention in support of the proposition that Australian Army veterans had been putting to the Morrison government for years: that we had a 'moral obligation' to offer visas and assistance to those Afghan locals who had provided support on the ground for our deployed soldiers during the twenty-year war that ended in ignominy in August 2021. It was an important intervention from the Liberal Party's supreme Elder Statesman, who has managed to retain a reputation for electoral invincibility despite departing politics humiliated as the first prime minister to lose his seat since Stanley Bruce in 1929, but it was ignored.

The Afghans in question worked principally as interpreters, or 'terps', and had been threatened with retribution by the Taliban as a result of their efforts on our behalf.[24] Captain Jason Scanes was one of the Australian soldiers who fought for eight years to get the government to meet this moral obligation towards men who had risked their lives, eventually forming an organisation called Forsaken Fighters to lobby and raise awareness. He was appalled at the perfidy of a government that publicly and piously stated it was doing all that it could to assist the terps, while behind the scenes it was littering their path to safety with bureaucratic obstacles, including onerous paperwork and lengthy delays in processing and communication. Particularly galling was a strict legalism, decried by Howard, that excluded from dedicated visa programs—principally the Afghan Locally Engaged Employee program—those workers engaged as contractors rather than direct employees. After painstakingly pulling together the extensive paperwork required, many waited years to receive rejection letters from DFAT baldly stating that they were 'not considered an employee of one of the Australian government agencies identified under the legislative instrument'—this despite their applications containing letters of support from Australian soldiers who had worked alongside them.

After waiting for six years, a man known as Khalid had his application rejected on these grounds. With the media only now taking an interest in this long-running but hitherto little-noticed issue, Khalid received another letter saying he would now be admitted to Australia under a hurriedly established humanitarian program. But by then Kabul had fallen and Khalid and his family were in hiding. It is unclear if they were able to get to the airport before the final evacuation flights.[25] And they were not the only ones left behind. 'We will continue to do everything we can for those who have stood with us, as we have to this day,' Morrison said sombrely on 15 August 2021, words that flew in the face of the facts clinically presented by the veterans who had been ignored by both political leaders and departmental officers as they'd pressed the case for their mates. 'But,' continued Morrison, 'I want to talk openly to veterans that despite our best efforts, I know that support won't reach all that it should.'[26]

It seems unlikely that our best efforts, if seriously deployed over many years, could achieve nothing better than bureaucratic limbo for those endangered because of the assistance they'd provided to Australia in a theatre of war, yet there many languished. Only in the final weeks between the United States beginning to withdraw its troops and the fall of Kabul was any semblance of urgency on display, despite the government receiving advice weeks beforehand that bureaucratic delays were putting people at risk.[27] Even as the desperate thronged the airport, the government sought to cover its failings by listing the numbers it had managed to get out in such very difficult circumstances, which only served to reinforce how many more they could have saved if the commitment had been present in the relative calm of the months or years prior. As Scanes noted, the question was not how many terps were evacuated—answer: 1600 since 2013, including family members—but how many were left behind.[28] Until it was all too late, the government seemed yet again to be defining human beings, in this case our former brothers-in-arms, to whom we owed a debt of gratitude, as problems—furthermore, problems to dodge or manage, not solve.

On cue, several days after Morrison's hollow words, Peter Dutton appeared before the cameras to say those abandoned were probably terrorists anyway.[29] The first reports of a terp having been murdered by the Taliban came through on 10 October 2021.[30]

BE GRATEFUL WE DON'T SHOOT YOU

In her *Quarterly Essay* 'The Reckoning: How #MeToo Is Changing Australia', Jess Hill provides a compelling overview of the #MeToo movement in Australia. She describes its false start, and how it was nearly derailed by our anomalous defamation laws and News Corp's sloppy pursuit of Geoffrey Rush. But by March 2021, everything had changed. As Hill writes, 'three women— Kate Thornton, Grace Tame and Brittany Higgins—would trigger a resurgent #MeToo movement in Australia, and a citizen-led insurgency against the Morrison government'.[31]

The 2021 Australian of the Year Grace Tame is a remarkable force, a young woman who has lived through great trauma, a survivor of carefully planned and devastating sexual abuse who has emerged as a poised, powerful advocate for fellow survivors. Equipped with killer lipstick and one-liners, she is articulate and unapologetic, describing her own abuse, and, importantly, the grooming that preceded the assaults themselves, and thereby changing the conversation around child and sexual abuse. While her impressive advocacy only inspired the Morrison government to review the way our Australians of the Year are selected,[32] in others it fuelled courage.

One of those galvanised was former political staffer Brittany Higgins, who, watching an emotional Tame accept the Australian of the Year award from Morrison in January, was sickened by the hypocrisy of the Prime Minister lauding Tame for her bravery in speaking out when his government had sought to silence her.

Higgins had told her boss, then defence minister Linda Reynolds, of an alleged criminal violation at the hands of a colleague, Bruce Lehrmann. It was alleged to have taken place in Reynolds's ministerial office when Higgins passed out on a couch after a drunken night out. The way her allegation was handled by Reynolds, by her subsequent boss Michaelia Cash, their boss Morrison, and the many, many people who were told of the alleged crime committed against her, subsequently came under damning scrutiny.

Higgins was consistently treated as a political problem to be managed and silenced, rather than as a valued colleague. Despite the ever-growing list of people aware of Higgins's story, including senior members of and trusted fixers in Morrison's office, and despite the fact that journalist Samantha Maiden had submitted an extensive list of questions to that office the week prior, on 15 February Morrison told parliament with a barely straight face that he, along with the rest of Australia, only became aware of Higgins's allegations when he read them in the press that morning. No-one believed him. He then proudly reported that he'd needed his wife to impress upon him the seriousness of what had allegedly happened, describing the game-changing conversation he'd had with Jenny as if his ignorance and lack of empathy were commendable. The distress Brittany Higgins allegedly suffered was to Morrison relatable only in the context of the possibility his daughters could suffer a similar fate. If he'd been childless, presumably he would have remained indifferent, and if he'd had sons, well, who knows where his sympathies might have lain.

The third name Hill cited, Kate Thornton, belongs to a friend of mine. We became friends as precocious teenagers at that pivotal time when intense relationships are forged—some lifelong, some more transitory, but all invoking that seminal period when you feel you are on the edge of your life, preparing to take off, hoping to fly. Despite her brilliant mind and great talent, Kate never took off as expected. When we reconnected in July 2019, she told me why. She had fallen prey to a trauma that had not only kept her grounded but devastated her. She said she had been raped by attorney-general Christian Porter as a teenager in January 1988 and, despite her efforts to bury it, to move past it, she'd never recovered.

Kate had not told me of her suffering at the time, nor in the intervening decades when we'd fallen out of contact, but she was ready now to act, and she intended to report the alleged assault to the police. I was sick with fear for her about what lay ahead and the retributive intrusive media she would confront from the government's News Corp allies but offered her my unconditional support. She spoke to other friends from the time, marshalling her army. She engaged legal representation, the heroic team at Marque Lawyers, and had a preliminary meeting with NSW Police that led to the formation of Strike Force Wyndarra in the Child Abuse and Sex Crimes Squad. But upon her return to Adelaide in March 2020, her interactions with NSW Police stalled after deputy commissioner David Hudson refused the request of Wyndarra officers to travel to Adelaide to take Kate's statement, despite the travel having already been approved by three levels

statements—admissible in legal proceedings under the precedent of *Snyder v The Queen* in the Victorian Court of Appeal (April 2021). There were also sworn affidavits from witnesses that corroborated key details in Kate's statements and threw doubt on Porter's dismissive characterisation of the nature of their relationship. As I and other friends of Kate's became caught in a political and legal maelstrom that continues in fits and starts to this day, what I didn't expect to happen was nothing at all. I didn't anticipate that the only response would be untrue statements from the Prime Minister asserting Porter's exoneration from a police investigation that never began,[33] and meaningless repetition of the phrase 'the rule of law' as he determinedly did nothing about the fact that one of his senior ministers had been accused of rape. For all the talk of listening to women, it was the voice of the indignant accused that was heard on this matter, not that of his alleged victim, from her grave.

Morrison is simply ill-equipped to handle sensitive matters relating to gendered violence. He is uncomfortable around powerful women and oblivious to, and unconcerned about, sexism and inequity. In her biography of Morrison, *The Accidental Prime Minister*, Annika Smethurst writes of his attitude to women that 'broadly, he just doesn't seem to work constructively with them'. One female Coalition frontbencher described him to Smethurst as a 'deeply ingrained chauvinist'. Another male colleague said Morrison 'couldn't stand' some of his female colleagues, including Julie Bishop and Kelly O'Dwyer. There was consensus among several government ministers that 'Morrison simply prefers to work with other men'.[34] When, in March 2021, the women of Australia marched in their thousands demanding justice and freedom from violence, he told parliament how lucky we were that we were not being 'met with bullets', as we would be elsewhere.

It's the small things, I guess.

The disgust many women felt at the sleaze that engulfed the government showed up in a significant drop in their support in the polls, driven largely by women abandoning them.[35] Confronted with potential electoral fallout, Morrison finally took note and much was made of a hastily established and snappily titled new Cabinet Taskforce on Women's Equality, Safety, Economic Security, Health and Wellbeing, which comprised every female Cabinet minister, Morrison, Treasurer Frydenberg and, latterly and incredibly, Barnaby Joyce. At the time of the taskforce's formation in April, Morrison spoke volubly and emptily about its turbocharged agenda before giving the ladies a brief turn to talk. At the time of writing, it has achieved nothing. Later, the Morrison government rejected the central recommendation of the Australian Human Rights Commission's *Respect@Work* report: the 'positive duty' clause that would give employers a legal obligation to prevent sexual discrimination and harassment in the workplace, similar to the provisions of workplace health and safety laws intended to prevent injury. We currently wait with bated breath for their response to the *Set the Standard* report into the workplace culture of Parliament House. They've assured us that they will be 'taking action on all the recommendations,'[36] which is unlikely to be the same as implementing them.

LOSING THE RACE: RUDE, DISMISSIVE AND PENNY PINCHING

The first letter was sent in March 2020. Maari Ma Health Aboriginal Corporation, located in the small regional NSW town of Wilcannia, population 745, wrote to Minister for Indigenous Australians Ken Wyatt and pleaded with him to assist their community to prepare appropriately for what might come. 'Warnings from around the world are clear,' they wrote. 'The earlier we prepare and act, the better the outcomes will be. We cannot wait until the first case turns up in the community, or worse, the first hospital case presents.' The warnings in the message were ignored.

The second letter was sent in August 2021 as the Delta variant took hold in the community, this time addressed to Scott Morrison, with copies sent to then NSW premier Gladys Berejiklian and Health Minister Greg Hunt. It begged the Prime Minister to take control of the 'unfolding humanitarian crisis' as nearly 20 per cent of the local population tested positive to the virus, and overcrowded and poorly maintained housing made physically isolating a challenge.[37]

In lieu of assistance, NSW Health Minister Brad Hazzard said the residents were to blame for attending a funeral in breach of health restrictions. He had to apologise two days later when it was revealed there had been no breaches of health orders at the Wilcannia funeral, which occurred before that part of the state went into lockdown.[38] And when their one supermarket closed with empty shelves and people were left without food supplies, authorities told them to ring Uber Eats.[39] It was left to the community to fundraise to ensure people had enough to eat.

Far from being an isolated example, Wilcannia's fate was emblematic of the neglect of the country's most vulnerable people. Despite being in the A2 priority group—second in line—the vaccination rate within Aboriginal communities remains to this day well below the national average, still playing catch-up after the early catastrophic problems with supply and distribution. As the government fell behind in their vaccine rollout, instead of trying to fix the problem, they quietly dropped entire categories of vulnerable people from their priority lists.[40] The closest that Indigenous peoples got to being vaccinated at the front of the queue, as promised, was when the handful of Indigenous boarders at Sydney's wealthy private school St Josephs were used as an excuse to get all 163 boarders vaccinated with Pfizer. This was at a time when people under forty weren't eligible for Pfizer at all, and aged-care residents and other vulnerable members of the so-called A1 group—the quarantine and border workers, frontline health officials, and aged-care and disability-care workers and residents—were still waiting.

Early in the pandemic, Norman Swan broke the big story that, in June 2020, Pfizer had begged us to take millions of doses of their coveted vaccine, but Greg Hunt wouldn't take their meeting. He sent bureaucrats in his place who either lacked the authorisation or the confidence to negotiate a deal, and instead nickel-and-dimed the in-demand Pfizer executives and squabbled over the signing of a non-disclosure agreement. Hunt, however, emphatically denied there were ever additional vaccines on offer, faster. 'Your presumption there is incorrect about Pfizer contacting Australia,' Hunt said to *Four Corners* journalist Adam Harvey. Harvey pushed back: 'Pfizer say they had contacted Australia.' 'No,' insisted Hunt.[41] He later added: 'The error in what you're suggesting is that we could have had more supply earlier … the capacity to deliver has been at the maximum level under the Pfizer contract.'[42]

Hunt kept denying Swan's claims, even as accounts of the botched early Pfizer approaches periodically emerged, including when Kevin Rudd popped up to describe with gravitas and glee the Zoom call he'd had with Pfizer's CEO and chair at the behest of some worried businessfolk. Hunt continued to ridicule the very idea that more vaccines might have arrived, and sooner. With the advent of Delta on our shores and the ensuing lengthy lockdowns in our biggest cities, things turned very sour, and the vaccine 'strollout' became the biggest political issue of the day. Following a freedom-of-information (FOI) application by Labor, the government was forced to release documents confirming that what Swan had reported was entirely accurate: there *had* been an invitation from Pfizer to be at the front of the queue, and Pfizer had been badly offended when the government fobbed off the task to junior bureaucrats who had, according to one source, adopted a 'rude, dismissive and penny pinching' approach.[43] The Pfizer reps packed up their contracts for bountiful vaccines and went home.

Astonishingly, Hunt continued to deny these facts even though they were outlined in the official government papers he'd tried to hide, as if we could be distracted from the words on the pages we were reading, or persuaded they meant something else. With Pfizer barely trickling in, and AstraZeneca the poor cousin after Morrison lost his nerve and undermined its credibility with dramatic late-night press conferences warning of blood clots, and restricting the age of those eligible to receive it, the vaccination timetable slipped further and further behind. Instead of taking action to rectify it, Morrison first said everything was fine, then that COVID was a nimble bitch with all these new variants, and who could keep up? Then the targets were abandoned altogether. Occasionally we woke to the exciting news that a dawn flight out of Warsaw or Sofia was winging its way to us carrying extra doses of freedom.

On 17 November 2021, a weary and angry Australia was emerging out of what was promised to be the final lock-downs, with nearly 80 per cent of the eligible population vaccinated. Morrison was touring the country doing such important work of state as getting a haircut and making gnocchi, with the media on hand to take his selfies, and proclaiming, as his deputy had before him from a paddock back in December 2019, that everyone just wanted the government out of their lives. As he did, we learned Delta had made it into remote Aboriginal communities for the first time. With the national Indigenous vaccination rate still below 55 per cent, the Binjari and Rockhold communities outside Katherine in the Northern Territory went into a snap, hard lockdown. Those away from the community at the time found themselves with nowhere to go.

I AM, YOU'RE NOT, WHO IS AUSTRALIAN?

Julian Assange sought to be the conscience of the world. A pretentious aim, perhaps, but noble, and Assange was prepared to put real skin in the game. A direct link could be drawn from his early days of hacking to the establishment of the anarchic WikiLeaks, with Assange relishing his role as its public face. With a courageous if cavalier approach to consequences, he took on the most powerful people in the world. Since the dramatic screening of the *Collateral Murder* video in 2007, which showed the brutal gunning down of Reuters' journalists in Baghdad by American soldiers treating it as sport, Assange and WikiLeaks have broken more major stories than any other single person or organisation. And for that, he has been hunted and, despite being convicted of no crime, has spent more than two years imprisoned in maximum security in Britain's Belmarsh, his mental health in freefall, his life imperilled, the very real risk of death by suicide the only thing preventing him from being handed over to the regime that plotted to assassinate him.[44]

Through it all, our government has forsaken him. The only reference Scott Morrison has made to Assange since his ordeal began after seeking asylum in the Ecuadorean Embassy in London in June 2012, to escape extradition to Sweden on some compromised charges of sexual assault from whence he feared extradition to the United States, was when Morrison made lewd and sexist jokes about Pamela Anderson after she made representations for justice on Assange's behalf. Assange's Australian citizenship seems without value or meaning as the US Government seeks to make an example of him.

The import of Australian citizenship has been under close scrutiny throughout the pandemic. We watched in fear as the virus swept the world, and we moved quickly to capitalise on our island status and keep the disease at bay. Our international borders were slammed shut in March 2020 and most foreigners were barred from entering entirely. Caps were put on Australian citizens and residents seeking to re-enter the country, mostly dictated by the number of hotel quarantine places available. The majority of the Australian population was broadly supportive of these measures: minimising the movement of people, whether traversing the globe or our cities, made immediate sense. The consequences of the policy dawned more slowly. As COVID-19 tightened its grip in Europe and the United States, many Australian travellers and expatriates who sought to return to the safety of their relatively disease-free homeland found themselves locked out, with the thousands of citizens and residents attempting to come home vastly outnumbering the numbers allowed into the country. Whenever there was an upsurge in local case numbers, state governments had a habit of slashing their international intake—when Delta took hold in Sydney in early July 2021, numbers were halved from a weekly high of 6075 to 3035 overnight.

So, despite seeing ourselves as a nation of globe-trotting adventurers, we had no compunction about abandoning our fellow Australians trapped overseas to their fate. The government's original reassurance that their travails would last only while we prepared for their return by boosting quarantine capacity and flattening the curve, proved hollow. No effort was made to build more quarantine facilities, and the stranded Aussies were not home by Christmas. Wrote travel writer and global backpacker Ben Groundwater, 'We discovered that there are two tiers of Australian citizenship: "us", who are here, and "them", who aren't.'[45] It mattered little if the 'them' who weren't here were experiencing hardship or distress, financial or otherwise, or had family at home who needed them. The government may well have been touting its attempts to 'keep Australians safe', but this only applied to those already in Australia. The rest were on their own. Rather than asking 'What needs to be done to solve this problem?', the government's preferred modus operandi was again 'How little can we do in relation to this problem before we cop blowback?'.

Indian Australians copped it even worse. When Delta first hit the headlines, the government banned anyone from coming into the country from India at all, regardless of the availability of flights and quarantine caps, or citizenship and residency status. One pondered the worth of Australian citizenship if it could no longer be assured to grant you entry into Australia. Months later, Morrison attended the unveiling of a statue of Mahatma Gandhi and talked about the value of family to the Indian Australian community, blithely ignoring how he'd banned many of the families of that community from returning from India when no such ban had been introduced for citizens returning from other equally infected countries. He went on to advise that his wife liked wearing saris and doing Bollywood dancing.[46]

THE RAW POLITICS OF NOW

We should have an updated version of the Godwin Rule where, instead of a mention of the Nazis prompting the loss of an argument, a debate is lost by the first person to reach for Trumpism as a lazy catch-all for the decline of Western civilisation. His election wasn't a good sign for America, but it's worth noting that in 2016 a majority of 2 868 686 voted for Hillary Clinton, and in 2020 the majority for Joe Biden was 7 060 140. Most Americans weren't in favour of Trump's corrupt rule, and even now, as the followers of his cult continue to bray loudly, it's a small minority of sad, mad people who turn up to his rallies and indulge his dishonest yet still dangerous rants.

But if the world thought that the disaster of Trump and his dangerous flirtation with authoritarianism was over after the November 2020 US election, Trump had more surprises in store. Clinton predicted it in one of their 2016 presidential debates, noting that Donald Trump's favourite line of defence if he's losing is to claim the process is rigged, recalling his tweets about the corrupt Emmys when he failed to win an award for *The Apprentice*. As more mainstream Republicans increasingly embrace Trump's Big Lie that Biden is an illegitimate president, the party has also populated the state legislatures with those who would be less inclined to stand up to Trump should his bullying of local officials to find additional votes for him occur again. Many of these hyper-partisan Trump acolytes see the power to certify election results as one of their driving motivations to seek office.

Australia is not at that point. Our elections are governed by a mercifully non-partisan body in the Australian Electoral Commission. But we have entered a time when, as in the Trump age in America, our public life has been corrupted: dishonesty is endemic, and Morrison's disdain for the truth is unparalleled. As Bernard Keane notes in his book *Lies and Falsehoods*, 'outright, verifiable lying was once relatively rare' but now 'has become a standard element of political discourse', something which not only has devastating implications for our democracy but for public policy as well. Its brazenness is also shocking. Morrison lies about things even when it can be proven almost instantaneously that he is lying—when transcripts, audio recordings or footage exists of him saying or doing exactly the things that he insists he never said or did. Morrison may not promote a single Great Lie in quite the vein of a stolen election or the benefits of Brexit, but he does promote endless little lies, about things he's said or done, and about things he says Labor secretly want or intend to do.

Politics has always been a numbers game, but this government's brutal exercise of power seems unusually flexed only to its own end, to retain it, and to continue a rapacious distribution of its spoils only to those in their tribe. Loyalty is paramount and rewarded. There's an assumption that the rules don't apply to them because they can use their numbers to shirk and flout, dodge and deceive, and instruct those within their sphere of influence to do the same if they wish to receive government largesse. They treat sovereign money as their own. They hand it unchecked to third parties via subsidies or preferred tenders, such as when the shelf companies Paladin and Canstruct were offered billions to work in our offshore detention centres. They approve inexplicably generous deals, such as the Leppington Triangle land purchase, or hand money to organisations that didn't ask for it, such as the Great Barrier Reef Foundation. They deploy infrastructure funds in Coalition held or targeted seats in brazenly partisan, inequitable and often unnecessary expenditure: North Sydney and Double Bay are temporarily reclassified to enable regional development funds to flow their way.[47]

There's also a propensity to disparage and delegitimise those who oppose or obstruct them, including important institutions. The Independent Commission Against Corruption (ICAC) becomes a kangaroo court for investigating Gladys Berejiklian. The AAT is stacked to prevent judgments that challenge government policy. Ministers attack and ignore court rulings and retreat from any kind of accountability. They reduce the funding and capacity of the Australian National Audit Office (ANAO), which first raised the issue of the government's rampant pre-election misuse of public funds with the release of the January 2020 report *Award of Funding under the Community Sport Infrastructure Program*. That report went on to trigger the first use of the now-infamous Gaetjensian Shield, whereby any contentious issue for the government is shunted off to an inquiry led by Phil Gaetjens, the Secretary of the Department of Prime Minister and Cabinet, heralded as an upstanding public servant ideally placed to investigate contested allegations, but actually a political warrior and ally of the Prime Minister, having served as chief of staff to Peter Costello for ten years and Scott Morrison for three. They refuse to release information under FOI requests and take questions on notice at Senate Estimates that never get answered. They favour 'word salads' at Question Time and press conferences, where endless random words are thrown together in deadening ways. All of this demonstrates a singular antipathy to transparency that manifests in the regular assertion of the right to non-disclosure, merely a ruse to dodge accountability—you can't be held to account for things you do or say you'll do if you refuse to tell anyone what you've said and done.

It is not hyperbolic to say that under Morrison we have entered a Trumpian era, albeit one governed by a uniquely Daggy Dad–infused Australian Way. We float in a post-truth world with a leader shrewdly playing the clown, as

Boris Johnson does in the United Kingdom. In response to violent protests against vaccination mandates, Morrison is happy to proclaim that he 'understands people's frustration' at too much government in their lives, even as protestors pull gallows down Melbourne's Spring Street while shouting threats against elected officials. There are no consequences for such behaviour: on 20 October 2021, the Morrison government voted down a motion recommended by the respected speaker Tony Smith to refer Christian Porter to the Privileges Committee, to examine the issue of a slush fund into which monies had been donated on which Porter could draw to cover the costs of the multi-strand, ill-fated litigation in which he had inveigled himself. Porter asserted that he knew nothing of the origin of the funds, and that as a 'potential beneficiary' he had no access to information about it. A vast wad of cash—amount and source unknown— would simply parachute into his bank account and the government required no further disclosure from him about it.

In a news interview, a horrified Geoffrey Watson, the former counsel assisting NSW ICAC and a current director of the Centre for Public Integrity, listed the risks with the government's position:

> One: you've harmed the reputation of parliament; Two: You've undermined the independence of the Speaker; Three: You've confined or restricted parliament's ability to scrutinise the conduct of its own members; and Four: you've engaged in a cover-up.

He added: 'Something has gone wrong with this government … This is a very black day for Australian parliamentary history.'[48]

Like Morrison himself, Australia is becoming less than the sum of its parts as our Prime Minister seeks to remake us in his own image. Sean Kelly notes in his illuminating book *The Game: A Portrait of Scott Morrison* that 'Morrison is willing to turn other people's misfortune, and his role in that misfortune, into a stunt with which to advance his career'.[49] We have stopped being a serious nation, a sober global citizen who works with other nations for the betterment of the world, mindful of others, the planet, the future. We are instead a shallow, venal, self-serving country that cannot be trusted to keep its word, and that takes the worst kind of domestic politics to the international stage.

When Morrison was accused of lying by France's President Emmanuel Macron over the cancellation of the Naval Group submarine contract, our wave of embarrassment was accompanied by the small, frustrated fillip of 'Now you know what it's like for us'. The difference is we brought this on ourselves.

We have a government defined by dishonesty of epic, now global proportions, and with that comes national dishonour.

In her article *The Bad Guys are Winning*, Anne Applebaum writes about the circle formed by the new club of autocrats in countries such as Russia, China, Belarus, Iran, Cuba, Venezuela and Turkey. Autocracy Inc, she calls it, with countries run not just by one guy but by 'sophisticated networks composed of kleptocratic financial structures, security services and professional propagandists'. Rather than ideology, the members of this club are held together by a 'common desire to preserve and enhance their personal power and wealth'.[50] Today's modern tyrants don't care as much about breaking down Western boycotts because they're happy doing business with each other. They don't care what people think, either. Whether it's the Taliban, the Cuban security services or the Russian Federal Security Service, writes Applebaum, 'their goals are money and personal power. They are not concerned … about the happiness or well-being of their fellow citizens, let alone the views of anyone else.'[51]

Similarly, our friends in the Carbon Club share a common desire to keep making money, and they are happy to ride roughshod over the greater good to do so— exploring, drilling, mining and exporting fossil fuels as the planet burns; creating wealth, and the circumstances to create more wealth. With a leader in constant motion, searching for the best backdrop for his next selfies, policies are measured only in terms of those most likely to win the next election, and the Morrison government continues to do the bidding of the Club. They then convert a little of the money gifted to them by the government into donations, taxpayers' money now the Liberals'—like magic, or that software scam of theirs, Parakeelia.

And so the virtuous circle turns.

When the noble motivation to hold public office is lost, and the power and the confirmation of one's own superior status, whether conferred by God or otherwise, is all one pursues and venerates, we're in trouble. Paul Keating said leadership requires courage and imagination. We are failing at both, and at competence and commitment, too, with a lazy government, led by a lazy man, which lacks the willingness and capacity to put in the work.

Our current leadership can't even imagine a future that has already begun. Morrison hid the presentation Emergency Management Australia gave at the 5 November meeting of the so-called National Cabinet, a label given to a heads-of-government meeting in an attempt to shield it with Cabinet confidentiality, a fiction given the lie by the imperilled Administrative Appeals Tribunal. The briefing provided a comprehensive outline of the extreme weather events Australia is likely to experience in 2021–22. Storms, bushfires, cyclones, heatwaves, floods: they're all ahead of us over the next twelve months, something of an inconvenient truth when your message of sunny optimism and business as usual is all we need as the technology will save us, when you insist we don't need to change.

When the facts don't fit your political narrative, hide the facts. Dismiss the facts. Deny the facts even exist at all.

THE FLICKERING LIGHT ON THE HILL

Paul Keating's appearance at the National Press Club on 9 November 2021 was a blast of intellect and analysis to which we were no longer accustomed, a polemical, powerful critique of the recherché foreign policy of the Morrison government that has seen them retreat from active engagement with our region back into the embrace of earlier Anglospherical allies. Morrison and Dutton had started blithely beating the drums of war against China for domestic political consumption, in keeping with Morrison's inability to do anything without the next election in mind, regardless of the implications. Keating's address was a scathing takedown of the newly minted committee that is AUKUS, our crumbling relationship with China, and the failure of the ALP to grapple with either in a meaningful and realistic way. Labor had, he said, singling out Penny Wong, opted for a 'reasonably quiet political life' by ensuring there isn't 'an ounce of daylight between [her] and the Liberal Party'. Keating's interlocutor at the Press Club, Laura Tingle, whose eyebrows have been lauded as a more effective Opposition leader than Anthony Albanese, noted that Labor had its own three-word slogan to match the fatuous platitudes of Morrison: 'We're with them.'

Even the most die-hard of Labor supporters are unlikely to claim that, since Keating slipped out of parliament after his devastating defeat to Howard in 1996, the party has been visionary. The procession of leaders hasn't been able to weave a narrative for our country or times that inspires. The only one that got elected from opposition did so by promising to be Howard-lite: Howard without 'spending like a drunken sailor'. Kevin from Queensland was here to help, to be Howard without the baggage. On the night of his historic victory in 2007, Kevin Rudd allowed his excited supporters could 'have a strong cup of tea if you want, even an Iced VoVo on the way through. But the celebration stops there.' This was no time for joy or jubilation—there was work to be done. Even through a television screen, you could feel the excitement ebb from the room, as it did across the country as the nation understood their new prime minister was more 'Tintin meets the Rain Man' than inspirational leader.[52] The champagne went flat in an instant. The party was over before it began.

And so it proved.

Yet even the most sceptical of ALP supporters could not have predicted the debacle that was to come. After working so hard to return to the government benches after eleven punishing years of a Howard government that deliberately unleashed the dark demons of division, Labor squandered everything in six short years. On the night the knives were sharpened against Kevin Rudd, consigning him to history as the first prime minister to be summarily dismissed in their first term in office, Anthony Albanese noted despondently that by such actions his colleagues would fatally damage two Labor prime ministers.

And so it proved.

Whether perched on the front- or backbench, Rudd was a malevolent force throughout Julia Gillard's term as prime minister, plotting and scheming and leaking and fomenting, and the sheer persistence of his perfidy eventually brought Gillard down. Rudd's return to the leadership was never going to be enough to save Labor at the next election, and it was duly swept away by a reputation for chaos and self-obsession to which Rudd was the chief contributor. Despite this, he was oddly cheerful on election night 2013, his speech of concession more buoyant than his speech of victory six years before.

However briefly, he had been restored to his rightful position as prime minister, and if the nation had been condemned to an Abbott government to achieve that, it was a price Rudd was happy for us to pay.

Through the chaos and disillusionment of Labor's interregnum, some achievements. We ratified Kyoto, established the National Disability Insurance Scheme, put a price on carbon. The Apology. But there was also shame and missed opportunities. The capitulation to miners who refused to pay a share of the profits they gained from excavating our sovereign wealth. Leaving refugees to rot indefinitely in the gulags we paid our impoverished neighbours to host. The recategorisation of single parents into poverty. The refusal to countenance gay marriage because of, we were told, feminist principles, and definitely not as payback to the shoppies in Queensland.

No-one ever seemed all that enthused by the leadership of Bill Shorten. The powerful national secretary of the Australian Workers' Union (AWU) came to national prominence in the aftermath of the Beaconsfield Mine collapse, when, on Anzac Day 2006, seismic activity endangered the seventeen men working in the mine. Fourteen escaped immediately; one, Larry Knight, was tragically killed; two remained missing as Shorten immediately flew to Tasmania. He was there on Day 6 of the rescue operation when Todd Russell and Brant Webb were discovered alive but trapped. As the mine owners fumbled their initial response and communicated with the media by press release from Sydney, Shorten stepped smoothly into the breach, providing regular updates on the two men underground. 'The reality is, unions often know what's going on before other people, because these people are our members,' he said.[53] He was there for his members when all hope was thought lost and he rode the wave of euphoria as Russell and Webb strode out of the mine fourteen days after the original rockfalls.

Australia embraced him then, Bill Shorten, this straight-talking union leader in a chambray shirt and AWU bomber jacket. Entering parliament the following year, he rose swiftly through the ranks, promoted immediately to the frontbench and earning a reputation for diligent work in his portfolios. But he sacrificed his good blokeyness when he was instrumental in bringing down first one and then a second prime minister. Australians watched his flexing of factional power with suspicion and distaste, unimpressed by the disloyalty and overreach. When he defeated Anthony Albanese and became leader of the Labor Party after the demise of the second Rudd prime ministership in 2013, he wasn't greeted with a great wave of enthusiasm. This was the first leadership contest decided under new rules instituted in July 2013 as part of a suite of changes Rudd instigated to ensure leaders could not be as easily dispatched as he had been in 2010. The new rules required 60 per cent of the Caucus to support a leadership spill and then mandated a ballot of the party membership on any contested spills, with a 50:50 weighting given to each of the votes of the parliamentary and party members. Despite winning just shy of 60 per cent of the nearly 30 500 members' votes cast, it was not enough for Albanese to overcome Shorten's 55:31 advantage in

After defeat at the 2019 election, however, Shorten joined the ranks of Labor leaders who never became prime minister, his destiny denied. Many reasons have been posited for this, including the perennial criticism that Labor neglected its traditional working-class voters and became captive to its progressive middle-class supporters. Shorten expressed his regret that people 'saw some of our policies as being green-left, not for the worker'.[54] Labor had in fact taken a suite of policies to the election that should have appealed to working-class supporters: pulling back on the tax distortions in the housing markets via reform of negative gearing, halving the capital gains tax reduction, and saving billions in middle-class welfare by phasing out franking credits. But these targeted and equitable reforms informed a massive Morrison scare campaign that Labor seemed incapable of rebuffing—the 'death tax' scare proved impressively cold revenge for the Mediscare of 2013.

Shorten was also unable to weave the 284 policies Labor had costed into a persuasive narrative. The official ALP post-election review conducted by Craig Emerson and Jay Weatherill found that not only were voters over-whelmed by Labor's 'cluttered policy agenda', they saw through its attempts to walk on both sides of the street on climate and coal, in particular regarding support of Adani's Carmichael coalmine in Queensland. Shorten had claimed opposition to the Adani mine during the Batman by-election in March 2018, when Labor was under siege from the Greens, but the report notes that thereafter 'Labor hedged between not supporting the Adani mine outright while not opposing it outright, leaving it exposed to allegations of mixed messaging.'[55]

The Liberals and the Nationals make a fine art of not just mixed but contradictory messaging all the time, each liking to pretend they are not part of the same government as the other when particular policy positions don't align with that of their electorates. So-called moderate Liberals speak out against the Religious Discrimination Bill, and the deputy prime minister disavows the government's commitments under the COP26 pact, stating, 'The Nationals did not sign it. I did not sign it.'[56] This illogical behaviour, and the fact the two parties coexist uneasily in order to retain government, seem to be accepted by both the media and voters. But when the Labor Party confronts factions that are equally divided on issues within its own ranks and is forced either to craft policy compromises that keep both quiet, often pleasing no-one, or disempower one side of the debate, alienating both parliamentary and rank-and-file members, it attracts accusations of division from opportunistic opponents and the media. Labor's persistent refusal to countenance governing in coalition with other progressive parties or individuals opens fronts on their left alongside the perennial right and leaves it exquisitely vulnerable to accusations of being fork-tongued when it tries to spin a message one way in the inner city and another in the coal belt of the Upper Hunter.

Shorten's unpopularity could not be ignored as a factor in Labor's defeat, effectively reinforced by the two-pronged, multimillion-dollar campaign waged against him by the Coalition and Clive Palmer. While Palmer's intervention was unprecedented, Shorten's reputation for untrustworthiness, caused by his betrayal of two leaders, was all his own doing. The first betrayal might have got lost in the crowd: Rudd was a hopeless leader and there was a growing feeling that something had to give even if the coup against a first-time prime minister had been drastic and unexpected. But Shorten could never transcend his betrayal of Gillard three years later and the sense it conveyed that his loyalty was only ever conditional, transactional and temporary.

Alas for them, the Australian people sought someone of more steadfast character in the 2019 election, but they ended up with Morrison instead.

TERTIUM NON DATUR: DODGING THE WEDGE

In an article for John Menadue's *Pearls and Irritations* public policy journal, Barry Jones outlines his reasons for teaming up with John Hewson as patrons on The Truth and Integrity Project to target the Morrison government's record on climate change and integrity matters. He laments the toothless excuse of an integrity commission promoted sporadically by Morrison in a futile bid to get the issue off the front pages. On climate change, he writes that 'Morrison is wicked, Barnaby Joyce pretends to be crazy, while Labor is timid and fearful'.[57]

Labor's fear is understandable. The Coalition has been ruthless in exploiting wedge politics since 2001 by reducing complex areas of critical public policy to crude, often misleading or inaccurate binaries complete with mandatory three-word slogans with which to prosecute their side. Wedge politics draws on Aristotle's Law of the Excluded Middle, that for every proposition, either it or its negation is true, thus if one side of an issue is right, then the other must be wrong and there is no in-between. It seizes on and frames issues exclusively to wield them as weapons, deliberately simplifying them to things one is for or against. Writing on the effectiveness of wedge politics in *The Atlantic*, Abdallah Fayyad observed: 'An issue that voters had not really formed an opinion on is suddenly framed in a way that makes it one of the most important topics of an election season.'[58] The nuance required to navigate policy in a complex world of competing geopolitical interests, global crises and domestic inequities is foresworn in favour of short-term political goals that in turn promote a polarising, oppositional brand of politics well suited to the hysterical pace of our media cycle. Issues are weaponised rather than tackled. There's no middle ground.

Labor's solution to this has been to cleave ever more firmly to the Coalition on issues they fear may be turned against them. This leaves many voters disillusioned, frustrated at the lack of policy differentiation on critical matters. In the past, this disengagement saw voters stick with the status quo, proving the truth of Don Dunstan's declaration: 'If you're always afraid of losing votes, you'll never get out there and win them.'

It's possible that, by the time you read this, Labor will have announced an ambitious suite of policies that sets out a clear and inspiring vision; that acknowledges the clear and present danger facing our country and the world due to climate change, and calmly and courageously accepts the role Australia must play in correcting course; that sets out to persuade and to lead and win votes rather than cower at the prospect of losing them. Albanese is held to be an authentic Labor hero, brought up in a housing commission flat by a single mother to whom he remains devoted, and whose favourite pastime is fighting Tories just as he fought the Labor right in his hard factional days in Sydney's Sussex Street. True Believers remain hopeful that Albanese will step up and give the kind of speech for which a swathe of the population is waiting, one that cuts through the bullshit and the lies and the corruption and the cowardice and speaks into the silence at the heart of our politics.

It might sound something like this:

My fellow Australians

The world is on fire. Our planet is burning. Business as usual is no longer an option. In the last fifteen years, with our dithering and our denialism and our downright irresponsibility, we have failed our children and we have failed ourselves. We have gambled with our children's future and the future of all those with whom we share this planet.

This will stop with a Labor government.

The Labor Party sought to begin the necessary transition to a decarbonised economy when we took the Carbon Pollution Reduction Scheme to the 2007 election. We have been committed to doing what needs to be done ever since, even if we sought to do it incrementally and without the urgency we now know is required. But we could not find a way to wrest vital discussions about our planet's future from the toxic politics in which they have been mired since Tony Abbott led the Opposition.

The new fight starts today. We put before you now the policies that are necessary to keep the increase in global temperature below the 1.5 degrees that we committed to in Paris, something universally accepted to be the limit if we're to maintain a habitable world. We commit to transforming Australia's status as an outlier in international politics that acts as a handbrake on what needs to be done, into that of a contributor, a collaborator, a leader.

We will join our fellow nations and grasp hold of history.

We must wean ourselves off our carbon addiction, both as consumers at home and as dealers to the rest of the world. We cannot in all conscience claim we are working to lower our emissions domestically while we export coal for others to burn elsewhere. The planet knows no borders. When our coal exports are added to our own emissions—as logically they should be—we are the sixth-largest emitter in the world.

We must be brave, and that starts with telling the truth of the cost of both action and inaction.

Jobs will be lost as our economy is transformed. Coalmines will close as we shift power generation to renewables, as we heed the call of the International

Energy Agency and leave our coal and gas in the ground. In the last year alone, Australia approved three new coal projects. The current government's 'gas-led recovery' is opening up new gas fields in the Beetaloo Basin, in Scarborough and elsewhere that will add literally billions of tonnes of emissions to the atmosphere. A collective madness has seized us if we think this is acceptable, possible, survivable.

The Morrison government has their slogans ready so they can pretend they are taking action. They are not. They mouth platitudes about regional communities as they let our land scorch and our reefs bleach, as they poison the water and sell off gigalitres of what's left to corporate interests, as they look out for their mates.

Labor is the party of the worker. We are the ones who will ensure that our fellow Australians in the regions are not left behind as we do what is necessary in both the cities and the bush to stabilise the Earth's temperature. We will enact generous transition plans and partner with the states and territories to transform our mining regions into sustainable hubs of clean, green economic development. We will support other regional communities by bolstering our university sector, so ravaged by the pandemic. We will rebuild our arts community, and thank our artists for the solace they brought us in dark times.

If the Labor Party wins the next election, we will live up to our highest ideals and fight for the Light on the Hill, our party's great objective which, in the words of the mighty Ben Chifley, 'we aim to reach by working for the betterment of mankind not only here but anywhere we may give a helping hand'.

We will immediately increase JobSeeker to $450 per week and we will review the punitive requirement that people apply for jobs that aren't suitable simply to meet arbitrary obligations that, despite their name, don't seem to be mutual. This is an investment in our fellow citizens that we can afford. Ensuring all welfare recipients can live in dignity is a choice we can make.

It is a choice we can make for others, too. We can provide support for women, those exhausted by the endless balance of caring and professional responsibilities; for men, so they can step up and be deeply involved in the lives of their families; for workers, exhausted by the precarity of their existence in a casualised workforce, or the gig economy, or a job with pay that's stagnated as the cost of living has not. We will make our workplaces and communities a safe place for all, free from violence, from harassment, from discrimination.

We will release refugees currently imprisoned in hotels into the community on appropriate bridging visas, and those still offshore will be allowed to go to New Zealand or brought to Australia. Unless there are compelling reasons to the contrary, those brought to or already here in Australia will be permitted to stay. We will establish a royal commission into what went on in our offshore prisons—the violence, the deaths, the gargantuan waste of money—and we will not shirk from examining how we got to this point, where we traduced ourselves and our reputation for political gain.

Trust and respect are hard-won and quickly lost. We will work hard to re-establish the Australian Government's reputation with the people it serves and those abroad, restoring a sense of pride in what it means to be Australian and taking our place as a good international citizen once more. We will rebuild relationships and use diplomacy to advance the cause of a peaceful, stable, cooperative world. We will introduce legislation to establish a National Integrity Commission, and with it we will transform our politics and the way they are practised. Money will be spent carefully and wisely and exclusively in the nation's interest. Our politicians will be held to the highest of standards, ethically and legally, demonstrating leadership and behaviours that embody the best of our country. We will always be open and honest with the electorate, telling you the unvarnished truth clearly and promptly.

To our Aboriginal and Torres Strait Islander brothers and sisters, we thank you for the generosity with which you offered us the Uluru Statement from the Heart, and we hold out our hands to you in friendship so that we can walk together on the trek across this great country you have invited us to join. We look forward to the ancient sovereignty of your peoples shining through as the best and fullest expression of Australia's nationhood. It is beyond time.

We are ready.

Labor is ready to lead. We ask for your trust and your vote.

Of course, it's equally possible that Labor will not say these things and will continue to be as small a target as possible in a desperate bid to avoid being wedged. Barry Jones is sceptical of the wisdom of this strategy, noting that since 1929, Labor has only won government from opposition on three occasions, and each victory followed strong advocacy on contentious issues. Whither a Labor platform, he asks, writing that Labor's fearful capitulation to dodge the wedge means this:

> Morrison says, in effect: 'I don't want Labor to raise the issues of setting an emissions reduction target for 2030, setting a price for carbon, questioning AUKUS and asking when the submarines will arrive or where they will be made, or a more humane refugee policy, or restoring progressive taxation to meet the needs of an ageing population, phasing out negative gearing to make housing more affordable, or weakening the Commonwealth public service.'
>
> Labor says: 'We never thought of raising these subjects, because we are out of practice in arguing a case.'[59]

This approach, as encapsulated in Tingle's arch summary—'We're with them'—is unlikely to be enough to inspire the Australian electorate. Despite a shopping list of commendable policies—free TAFE, cheaper child care, industrial reform of the gig economy—Labor's key message becomes little more than: 'We're not them, and authentic Albo is certainly not fake ScoMo, but we remain sufficiently like them that you don't need to worry.'

Faced with this drab choice, disenchanted centrist voters may have previously been inclined to disengage from the political process entirely, but the slow building of a new political movement in Australian politics provides an alternative. The protracted birth of the Community Independents movement over the last eight years could provide a different path for voters uninterested in picking the lesser of two evils within the current system, and who favour creating a different system entirely. Despite Labor's rejection of the idea of governing in coalition, it is conceivable that the 2022 election will deliver a hung parliament, and that Labor's only hope of forming government will be with the support of an independent crossbench.

And given Labor's paroxysms over key moral questions, would that be such a bad thing?

THE TIPPING POINT IS NOW

The event's line-up was formidable, and the audience at the 2021 Sydney Writers' Festival was expectant: Cathy McGowan, Annabel Crabb, Kate Ellis and Mehreen Faruqi in a discussion on 'Women in Politics' chaired by Clare Wright. It was a lively session, if also depressing, traversing the discrimination Faruqi and Ellis faced from opponents in the parliament, and in Kate's case, from within her own party. Faruqi described how difficult she found it to even enter Parliament House since it had been revealed as a house of harassment, bullying and assault. She told the audience that, despite her previous career in the highly masculine profession of engineering, she had 'never felt more marginalised and sidelined' than as a politician. For Faruqi, as a migrant brown woman, the parliament was a 'very lonely place'. Ellis described the 'unspoken code of not acknowledging the sexist and unfair treatment that has long bubbled away in the background of parliament'. She told the shocking story of a Liberal staffer, now a member of parliament, introducing himself by asking how many men she had fucked to get elected. Steeped in the post-production of her immensely enjoyable series *Ms Represented*, Crabb provided an historical perspective on women's quest for electoral representation.

But it was McGowan who stole the show with her rallying cry for more women to get involved in politics as independents, to follow in the footsteps of Zali Steggall, Rebekha Sharkie, Kerryn Phelps, Helen Haines and McGowan herself—to accept their voice, grasp their collective power, and get out there with courage and capacity to 'do the work that needs to be done for the country'. She advocated for a strong, independent and female crossbench. 'It can be done,' she said, exhorting the overwhelmingly female audience at Carriageworks to share her vision of an Australia whose citizenry, rejecting the status quo, got themselves elected to parliament to change it. She believed it possible. She had done it.

'This could change things overnight,' she said emphatically, gesturing at the despicable anecdotes that hung in the air. 'For too long, we have underplayed the power of our vote. We haven't been strategic.' She challenged the audience to be brave, 'to be the change you want to see'. If we do, she assured us, we can have 'women of quality and courage and capacity and principle holding the balance of power'. Politics is a numbers game, she said, and we needed to be deliberate and strategic and go out and get those damn numbers.

It was inspiring stuff from McGowan, delivered in a brisk, firm way, accompanied by invitations to get involved, to attend workshops coordinated by Women for Election Australia. Community-based politics runs somewhat in McGowan's family, with her sister Ruth a principal in the Women for Election organisation, and her brother-in-law Denis Ginnivan, niece Leah Ginnivan and nephew Ben McGowan all instrumental in her first campaign for Indi. Denis subsequently founded Voices for AU, which seeks to inspire grassroots involvement in democracy across the nation, and he travels the country tirelessly, through COVID lockdowns by Zoom and now in person, to share his experience of the success of the Indi campaign, offering it up as a model for people to get involved in their community and consider backing—or being—candidates for election.

The story of McGowan's success in Indi is well known. After frustration at the neglect of the seat by the unlikeable incumbent Sophie Mirabella, in September 2012 a group of locals formed the community organisation Voices for Indi. Supported by Melbourne-based group Indi Expats, they created a community-focused strategy to shake things up, with the aim of turning Indi into a marginal seat at the September 2013 election. With a commitment to ensuring Indi's 'electoral voice is heard and represented at the national level', they developed what became known as Kitchen Table Conversations. Interested individuals were trained to facilitate discussion between small groups in their networks, serving both to provide Voices for Indi with insight into the issues important to locals, and to seed the idea of the community supporting a grassroots independent candidate at the next election. Initially reluctant to stand herself, after urging from others, McGowan accepted she would be a competitive contender and 'began the process of reconciling (her)self to six months of campaigning'.[60] Although the initial objective had merely been to shock the Liberal Party out of complacency by dramatically reducing its margin, McGowan invested all that she could on the campaign trail and was rewarded by the narrowest of victories eleven days after election night, when final pre-poll and postal votes were counted. Against the odds, McGowan had defeated Mirabella by 439 votes and was going to Canberra.

At Al Gore's Asia-Pacific training for climate change advocacy, organisers promoted the idea of 'lighthouse projects'. Said one attendee, Jane, who went on to work on Zali Steggall's 2019 campaign, 'It is something new that then acts as a lighthouse for everyone else. There is something that is now possible that wasn't possible before.'[61] McGowan's victories in 2013 and 2016 became lighthouse projects for other electorates and community-based independents disgusted by the state of federal politics, particularly those frightened or ashamed of our inaction on the existential question of climate change. They inspired Kerryn Phelps to run as an independent in the Wentworth by-election in October 2018 triggered by the resignation of Malcolm Turnbull after his ousting from the prime ministership. Phelps's strong victory saw a swing of 20 per cent against the government, giving her 57 per cent of the two-party-preferred vote, and it marked the first time in the seat's 117-year history that it had been surrendered by the Liberal Party. It forced Morrison into minority government, with six crossbenchers holding the balance of power.

With the exception of long-term maverick conservative Bob Katter, the parliament's crossbenchers rallied to support Phelps's first foray into the legislative arena, the Migration Amendment (Urgent Medical Treatment) Bill 2018, the so-called Medevac Bill that provided critically sick refugees and people seeking asylum who were held in offshore detention with a pathway to be transferred to Australia for urgent medical treatment. Phelps worked on the bill with McGowan and Rebekha Sharkie of the Centre Alliance, the remnant of the Nick Xenophon Team that had also delivered Stirling Griff and now independents Rex Patrick and Tim Storer to the Senate—albeit in a convoluted way after Xenophon's resignation from running for the South Australian Parliament in October 2017, and Skye Kakoschke-Moore's forced resignation in November 2017 after falling foul of the s.44 crisis that engulfed federal parliament. Liberal defector and now independent Julia Banks was also an important supporter of the bill following her resignation from the Liberal Party in November 2018 in the aftermath of the coup against Turnbull. With Andrew Wilkie, the Greens' Adam Bandt and the Labor Party also on board, Phelps succeeded in passing amendments to a government migration bill, the first time a government had lost a vote on its own legislation in almost eighty years. It was also the first positive measure taken in the field of refugee law since the early days of Rudd's administration.

Morrison was apoplectic and the government immediately sought to gain political mileage from the bill's passage. 'Australia is back on the map for people smugglers,' said Peter Dutton on *7.30*. As a result of the bill, he said, there are people in detention 'that can come to our country from Manus or Nauru. People that have been charged with child sex offences or have allegations around serious offences including murder.' When pressed by host Leigh Sales as to how many people in offshore detention were accused or suspected of such crimes, Dutton refused to answer.

The passage of the amendments was a clear demonstration of the impact a committed and cohesive crossbench could have. While they could not form government, they showed that they could influence the national and legislative agenda. They could get things done.

The euphoria was short-lived. At the 2019 election, Kerryn Phelps narrowly lost her seat to Dave Sharma, a former ambassador to Israel who had run again after losing to Phelps at the by-election. It was a blow to the Independents' movement. Standing as an independent in Flinders against Greg Hunt, Julia Banks also failed in her bid to return to parliament. On the plus side, McGowan, after serving the two terms to which she'd earlier committed, had retired and been replaced by Helen Haines, marking the first time that a seat had passed from one independent to another. Haines was joined on the crossbench by impressive newcomer Zali Steggall, the Abbott slayer, but the independents no longer held the balance of power. The government repealed the Medevac Bill on 4 December 2019 after securing the support of independent Senator Jacqui Lambie in a secret deal, the terms of which remain unknown to this day beyond the fact that the government has failed to deliver on them.

Initially, each of the successful independent candidates elected in this new modern era also had a rallying local issue on which to campaign. Cathy McGowan ran strongly on the idea that Indi had been neglected by a complacent Liberal Party. She campaigned on the need for greater investment in infrastructure in the rural Victorian seat, particularly around the lack of rail services and track maintenance, and poor internet connections and mobile phone coverage. The personal unpopularity of Mirabella, who was nominated by Tony Windsor for the 'nasty prize' as the person he'd miss least in politics,[62] was also considered a factor in her defeat. Kerryn Phelps's by-election victory was a protest vote against the deposing of Turnbull, while her loss at the general election reflected the abatement of the electorate's fury. An articulate barrister and former Olympian, Zali Steggall may have been a candidate from Central Casting, but people in Warringah also voted for her because of who she was not—namely

The loss of our moral compass on refugees. Our criminal complacency around gendered violence and inequity.

Ackery's opponent in Hume is the perennially unpopular scandal magnet and fossil fuel enthusiast Angus Taylor, who holds his seat by a margin of 13 per cent. 'Can we win?' says Ackery, contemplating the challenge. 'We can win because there's a wonderful growing independents movement that has paved the way, so that we know how to act, and what things need to be done.'[64]

So far, the tactics of the so-called moderate Liberals have been to paint these fiercely independent and mostly formerly apolitical women as Labor or Green stooges. Tim Wilson described Daniel as a 'puppet whose strings they're yanking to dance to their Labor and Greens tune', someone who was 'backed by Big Tech climate activists who want to rig laws so they can increase their profits from higher energy costs to businesses and households'.[65] While stating he respected everyone's right to run, Angus Taylor said the independents' movement was 'just another front for green activists to play dress up as independents'.[66] Dismissing these centrist candidates, many of whom would have sat comfortably in the previously broad church of the Liberal Party, as radical activists or stooges seems a risky tactic. Speaking at her campaign launch in Wentworth, where she was introduced by Chair of the Clean Energy Finance Corporation and former Reserve Bank director Jillian Broadbent, Allegra Spender noted, 'Today's Liberal Party is not the same party as that of my father and grandfather.' She called out the attempts to undermine her independent credentials: 'Wentworth is not radical and I am not a

comes a new burst of enthusiasm. People are rejecting the notion that we have to accept business as usual
and that our government can only comprise one of two
major parties—three, if one includes the junior party of
the Coalition, the Nationals, which I suppose one must.
The candidates are receiving community support from
the 'Voices of' movement. Some are receiving logistical
and financial support from Climate 200, an organisation
set up by Simon Holmes à Court with the sole aim of
getting pro-climate independents elected and holding the
balance of power in a hung parliament.

Holmes à Court notes in regards to building on the
existing crossbench that 'if we can just win two or three
seats it's highly likely there will be a minority government'.
He rejects the accusation from under-threat Liberals
that the candidates are stooges of anyone, be it Labor,
the Greens or, as worried Member for Mackellar Jason
Falinski put it, 'big tech billionaires and trust fund kids'.
'We are not starting any campaigns,' Holmes à Court
says. 'We are helping to turbocharge them. They rise
up in seats where people feel very strongly they are
being misrepresented.'[69]

WHO'S AFRAID OF A HUNG PARLIAMENT?

The government may try and stoke fear at the prospect
of one party failing to win an absolute majority, but to do
so is the height of hypocrisy. The Liberal Party has never
ruled in its own right since its formation under Menzies,
relying on the Nationals to secure a majority. As historian

Judith Brett notes, while we have become so used to stable majority governments in Australia that 'minority governments are treated as disastrous aberrations and sure signs of political dysfunction, for the Commonwealth's first decade they were the norm'.[70] Our most successful early prime ministers led minority governments, with Alfred Deakin drawing support from wherever he could find it to secure the passage of his legislation, and Stanley Bruce negotiating the first formal coalition and the antecedent of the agreement between the Liberals and the Nationals today.

Many of our key trading partners and allies govern in coalition, too, sometimes comprising quite surprising members. Since the reunification of Germany in 1990 under the leadership of Helmut Kohl, a big man with a long shadow, the country has consistently been led by coalitions. Angela Merkel's Christian Democratic Union (CDU) only ever governed in coalition, often in so-called 'Grand Coalitions', with the CDU's main rival, the Social Democratic Party (SDP). Her successor, the SDP's Olaf Scholz, has just formed the next government in partnership with the Greens and the small Free Democratic Party.

Who can forget the 2017 election in New Zealand when Jacinda Ardern first came to office? When New Zealand's mixed-member proportional (MMP) system failed to deliver either the National or Labour parties an absolute majority, kingmaker Winston Peters of the New Zealand First Party kept Ardern and the incumbent government of the Nationals waiting for twenty-seven days as he cogitated on his choice. On 19 October, he announced that, despite

Ardern's Labour Party having only won forty-six seats to the Nationals fifty-six, New Zealand First would support it in coalition, with the Greens guaranteeing confidence and supply. This became New Zealand's first coalition government under MMP when the most popular party was not in government, something which proved no impediment to Labour's successful first term of government. It won office in its own right at the next election.

In Canada, minority governments are regularly formed, with the party with the most votes assuming power. They've had fifteen of them, of all varieties, which hasn't prevented Canada from being effectively governed. Canada's ruling party doesn't even bother to enter into formal coalitions with smaller parties but relies on negotiating a majority for the passage of each piece of legislation, something at which Julia Gillard was spectacularly successful during her time leading a minority Australian Government from 2010 to 2013. Despite the bad press generated by Tony Abbott's misinformation and Rudd's sniping, the Gillard government was the most productive since Federation when measured by the number of bills passed.[71] During the 2013 election campaign, the Opposition sought to capitalise on the false impression of an unproductive term by promising a 'grown-up government', ironically then delivering a government led by Tony Abbott (albeit temporarily).

The independents standing for office in the 2022 federal election are serious-minded, policy-driven, high-achieving professional women with a wide range of expertise and life experience, and it is difficult to see how their election to federal parliament would do anything other than enhance the legislative process. Committed to working collaboratively with each other and the government of the day to support sensible, centrist, evidence-based policy, they would inspire more confidence than whoever the latest round of major-party preselections may throw up, wedded as they must be to the talking points and bad or timid policies of their party HQs. In government, the Coalition seems only as clever as their dumbest link, and among the Nationals and LNP in particular, there are those that are daft as a brush.

In her book, *Twilight of Democracy: The Failure of Politics and the Parting of Friends*, Anne Applebaum documents how authoritarianism can take hold in a country. She also describes what is required for liberal democracy to flourish, with its constitutional checks and balances never proving enough. 'Liberal democracies always demanded things from citizens,' she writes. 'Participation, argument, effort, struggle.' And if things get difficult, if alternative visions of our nations try and draw us in, 'we will find that together we can resist them'.[72]

Said challenger Penny Ackery at her campaign launch: 'This is not just the launch for the independent candidate for Hume. This is also the relaunching, the rekindling, of our democracy.'

Sounds pretty good to me.

ACKNOWLEDGEMENTS

This year, 2021, has been one of tumult, for me, for many. To those who offered succour across this year's strange journey, I am grateful. Friends both very old and newly met have been invaluable. If there has been a silver lining in the deep sadness and high stress that have punctuated this year, it is you.

Adelaide Writers' Week has been a source of great joy. The authors who shared the thrill of a returning community in March were a stimulation and a salve. I thank my partner in crime, Suzanne Critchley, for her commitment to our cause and her bone-dry outlook. I could not be happier that Louise Adler, responsible for this book and such a force in Australia's literary and intellectual life, will be Writers' Week's new director when I step down in March.

Undaunted by lockdowns and border closures and quarantining and cancellations, my theatre community has provided solace, distraction and some bloody good shows. Thank God we're back.

To Tom and Ez, the chaos is real but the calm will come. Hold on! I am—for dear life.

I end the year with the decision to channel my frustration productively and be part of the campaign to change our country at the next election. As an independent candidate for Boothby, I am proud of the support offered to me by the Voices of Boothby and grateful for the advice and enthusiasm of Dennis Ginnivan.

The country needs a circuit-breaker. Please make your vote count in 2022.

NOTES

1   R Garnaut, *The Garnaut Climate Change Review*, Cambridge University Press, Canberra, 2008, p. 118.

2   Brent Hodgson, Twitter, 3 November 2021, https://twitter.com/BrentHodgson/status/1455871306675589126?s=20

3   IEA, 'Pathway to Critical and Formidable Goal of Net Zero Emissions by 2050 Is Narrow but Brings Huge Benefits', press release, 18 May 2021.

4   L Cozzi and L Gül, *Net Zero by 2050: A Roadmap for the Global Energy Sector*, IEA Special Report, May 2021, p. 14.

5   S Ludlum, *Full Circle: A Search for the World that Comes Next*, Black Inc, Melbourne, 2021, p. 263.

6   M Wilkinson, *The Carbon Club*, Allen & Unwin, Sydney, 2020, p. 13.

7   Michael West Media's *Revolving Doors* series (https://www.michaelwest.com.au/revolving-doors) documents the astonishing close ties between the fossil fuel industry and the Morrison government.

8   Matt Canavan's brother John is managing director of private coal company Winfield Energy.

9   *Sharma v Minister for the Environment* [2021] FCA 560, par 293.

10 Reuters, 'Australia Approves Third New Coal Mine Extension in a Month', 5 October 2021, https://www.reuters.com/business/energy/australia-approves-third-new-coal-mine-extension-month-2021-10-05

11 R Verschuer and H Melville-Rea, *What Is Australia Bringing to COP26?*, Australia Institute, Canberra, October 2021, p. 4.

12 350.org Australia, 'Gas-Tastrophe: The Climate Impact of the Government's Strategic Gas Basins', 2 February 2021, https://350.org.au/gas-tastrophe-the-climate-impact-of-the-governments-strategic-gas-basins

13 R Campbell, E Littleton and A Armistead, *Fossil Fuel Subsidies in Australia*, Australia Institute, Canberra, April 2021.

14 K Murphy and D Hurst, 'Scott Morrison "Did a Jig" Following Approval of $16b Gas Project Labelled a Disaster By Green Groups', *The Guardian*, 24 November 2021, https://www.theguardian.com/environment/2021/nov/24/scott-morrison-did-a-jig-following-approval-of-16bn-gas-project-labelled-a-disaster-by-green-groups

15 Josh Frydenberg, 'Tom Hughes Oration: COVID-19—Rising to the Challenge, Seizing the Opportunities', Sydney, 11 March 2021, https://joshfrydenberg.com.au/latest-news/tom-hughes-oration-covid-19-rising-to-the-challenge-seizing-the-opportunities

16 Andrew Charlton, National Press Club address, 17 November 2021.

17 D Hardaker and J Landis-Hanley, 'The Big Stack', *Crikey News*, 24 September 2019, https://www.crikey.com.au/inq/the-big-stack

18 David Graeber, Twitter, 26 April 2020, https://twitter.com/davidgraeber/status/1254405137994481667?s=20

19 *The Sydney Morning Herald*, 'Rear Admiral Bonser's Testimony', 28 May 2002, https://www.smh.com.au/national/rear-admiral-bonsers-testimony-20020528-gdfbhh.html

20 S Armbruster, 'SIEV X Anniversary: Cover-up Claims Remain 20 Years after 353 Asylum Seekers Drowned', *SBS News*,

19 October 2021, https://www.sbs.com.au/news/siev-x-anniversary-cover-up-claims-remain-20-years-after-353-asylum-seekers-drowned/19d01b23-c58f-40c5-b440-36c5cc2808c3

21 B Doherty and C Wahlquist, 'Government to Pay $70m Damages to 1905 Manus Detainees in Class Action', *The Guardian*, 14 June 2017, https://www.theguardian.com/australia-news/2017/jun/14/government-to-pay-damages-to-manus-island-detainees-in-class-action

22 M Knott and M Hasham, '"I Said Allegedly Barrie": Scott Morrison Refuses to Apologise to Save the Children', *The Sydney Morning Herald*, 8 May 2016, https://www.smh.com.au/politics/federal/i-said-allegedly-barrie-scott-morrison-refuses-to-apologise-to-save-the-children-20160508-gop1el.html

23 M McKenna, 'First Words: A Brief History of Public Debate on a New Preamble to the Australian Constitution, 1991–99', research paper 16, 4 April 2000, Parliament of Australia, Canberra, https://www.aph.gov.au/About_Parliament/Parliamentary_Departments/Parliamentary_Library/pubs/rp/rp9900/2000RP16

24 R Yosufzai, 'John Howard Says Australia Has a Moral Obligation to Help Afghan Interpreters', *SBS News*, 8 July 2021, https://www.sbs.com.au/news/john-howard-says-australia-has-a-moral-obligation-to-help-afghan-interpreters/ae1e14cb-d698-4168-8052-24d6cb358e04

25 M Muneeb and P Theodosiou, 'Afghan Interpreters Found "Eligible" for Australian Resettlement in Apparent Asylum Fast Track', *SBS Pashto*, 18 August 2021, https://www.sbs.com.au/language/english/afghan-interpreters-found-eligible-for-australian-resettlement-in-apparent-asylum-fast-track

26 G Hitch and S Dziedzic, 'Scott Morrison Admits that Government Cannot Help all Afghans who Helped ADF Stuck in Afghanistan', *ABC News*, 17 August 2021, https://www.abc.net.au/news/2021-08-17/scott-morrison-humanitarian-refugee-visa-afghanistan-taliban/100383784

27 D Hurst, '"Tragic" Delays: Documents Reveal Australia Knew Time Was Running out to Extract Afghan Staff', *The Guardian*, 1 December 2021, https://www.theguardian.com/world/2021/dec/01/tragic-delays-documents-reveal-australia-knew-time-was-running-out-to-extract-afghan-staff

28 P FitzSimons, '"He Could Have Done Something": Why Diggers Feel Let Down by Scott Morrison', *The Sydney Morning Herald*, 22 August 2021, https://www.smh.com.au/national/he-could-have-done-something-why-diggers-feel-let-down-by-scott-morrison-20210820-p58kks.html

29 D Hurst, 'Peter Dutton Suggests Some Former Afghan Guards and Interpreters Could Pose Security Risk to Australia', *The Guardian*, 18 August 2021, https://www.theguardian.com/australia-news/2021/aug/18/peter-dutton-suggests-some-former-afghan-guards-and-interpreters-could-pose-security-risk-to-australia

30 T Skelton, H McDonald and K Browning, 'Afghan Interpreter Who Worked with Australian Troops Murdered by Taliban', *ABC News*, 20 October 2021, https://www.abc.net.au/news/2021-10-20/afghan-interpreter-worked-with-australian-troops-killed-taliban/100552634#

31 J Hill, 'The Reckoning: How #MeToo Is Changing Australia', *Quarterly Essay*, Black Inc, Melbourne, 2021, p. 91.

32 K Middleton, 'Government Review Follows Tame Appointment', *The Saturday Paper*, 1–7 May 2021, https://www.thesaturdaypaper.com.au/news/politics/2021/05/01/exclusive-government-review-follows-tame-appointment/161979120011566

33 A key finding from the Post Operational Assessment of Strike Force Wyndarra, established to investigate Kate's allegations, were that they 'never had the opportunity to commence the investigation into the historical sexual abuse of [Kate] due to her passing by suicide': p. 6.

34 A Smethurst, *The Accidental Prime Minister*, Hachette Australia, Sydney, 2021, p. 332.

35 S Martin, 'Women Abandon Coalition with Fewer than One in
    Three Backing It, Essential Poll Shows', *The Guardian*, 29 April
    2021, https://www.theguardian.com/australia-news/2021/
    apr/29/women-abandon-coalition-with-fewer-than-one-in-
    three-backing-it-essential-poll-shows

36 Josh Frydenberg interview with David Speers, Insiders, ABC,
    5 December 2021.

37 J Kennedy, 'Leaked Letter Warns of COVID Disaster in Aboriginal
    Community in Wilcannia 18 Months Ago', *ABC News*, 31 August
    2021, https://www.abc.net.au/news/2021-08-31/letter-warned-
    government-of-covid-disaster-in-wilcannia/100420052

38 C von Hörchner, 'The Covid Disaster Unfolding in Wilcannia
    Goes Way Past Incompetence. It Is a Disgrace', *Barrier Daily
    Truth*, 25 August 2021, https://bdtruth.com.au/main/news/
    article/12364-Wilcannia-abandoned.html

39 K Jenkins, 'Wilcannia Families Struggle to Isolate in
    Overcrowded Houses', *NITV*, 24 August 2021, https://www.sbs.
    com.au/nitv/article/2021/08/24/wilcannia-families-struggling-
    isolate-overcrowded-housing

40 B Rolfe, 'People with Disabilities Bumped from Phase 1A of
    Vaccine Rollout as Aged Care Received Priority', *news.com.au*,
    29 September 2021, https://www.news.com.au/world/
    coronavirus/australia/people-with-disabilities-bumped-from-
    phase-1a-of-vaccine-rollout-as-aged-care-received-priority/
    news-story/5692eb1cf3451d7d9352106ca902d51c

41 A Harvey, 'Vaccinating Australia: What Went Wrong?', *Four
    Corners*, ABC, 24 May 2021, at 9:48.

42 Ibid., at 19:20.

43 L Tingle, 'Senior Business Figures Turned to Former PM
    Kevin Rudd to Intervene in Bringing Forward Australia's Pfizer
    Vaccine Supply', *ABC News*, 11 July 2021, https://www.abc.
    net.au/news/2021-07-11/kevin-rudd-australia-covid-pfizer-
    vaccine-supply-senior-execs/100284902

44 Z Dorfman, SD Naylor and M Isikoff, 'Kidnapping,
    Assassination and a London Shoot-out: Inside the CIA's Secret

War Plans against WikiLeaks', *Yahoo News*, 26 September 2021, https://au.news.yahoo.com/kidnapping-assassination-and-a-london-shoot-out-inside-the-ci-as-secret-war-plans-against-wiki-leaks-090057786.html

45 B Groundwater, 'Australia International Borders Opening, but Travellers and Expats Should Not Forget How They Were Treated', *Traveller*, 6 October 2021, https://www.traveller.com.au/australia-international-borders-opening-but-travellers-and-expats-should-not-forget-how-they-were-treated-h1yzqo

46 Scott Morrison, 'Remarks at Australian Indian Community Centre, Rowville, Victoria', 12 November 2021, https://www.pm.gov.au/media/remarks-australian-indian-community-centre-rowville-victoria

47 The redevelopment of the North Sydney Olympic Pool and the purchase of a safety vessel for the Double Bay Sailing Club were part-funded by Commonwealth grants from the Regional Development Fund: see https://www.grants.gov.au/Ga/Show/1319bf7d-2b25-4ff8-ac0f-e794c28885a6 and https://www.grants.gov.au/Ga/Show/50983a1b-9a31-1a2e-c7d5-570360662016

48 Geoffrey Watson interview with Joe O'Brien, *ABC News 24*, 21 October 2021.

49 S Kelly, *The Game: A Portrait of Scott Morrison*, Black Inc, Melbourne, 2021, p. 20.

50 A Applebaum, 'The Autocrats Are Winning', *The Atlantic*, 15 November 2021, https://www.theatlantic.com/magazine/archive/2021/12/the-autocrats-are-winning/620526/

51 Ibid.

52 A description Jonathan Biggins puts into the mouth of Paul Keating in his play *The Gospel According to Paul* (2019).

53 B Doherty, 'Shorten Plays More than Mere Union Man', *The Age*, 4 May 2006, https://www.theage.com.au/national/shorten-plays-more-than-mere-union-man-20060504-ge28wv.html

54 R Lewis and R Baxendale, 'Bill Shorten: I Misread the Mood in Queensland and Western Australia', *The Australian*, 6 October

2019, https://www.theaustralian.com.au/nation/politics/bill-shorten-admits-labor-loss-was-all-his-fault/news-story/3f788 9851386fef0b4a090fd5bd299a3

55 C Emerson and J Weatherill, 'Review of Labor's 2019 Federal Election Campaign', Australian Labor Party, 2019, p. 35.

56 Barnaby Joyce interview with Patricia Karvelas, *Afternoon Briefing*, ABC, 22 November 2021.

57 B Jones, 'A Unity Ticket to Challenge the Integrity Vacuum in Canberra', *Pearls and Irritations*, 25 November 2021, https:// johnmenadue.com/a-unity-ticket-to-challenge-the-integrity-vacuum-in-canberra

58 M Petersen and F Fayyad, 'The Irresistible Effectiveness of Wedge Politics', *The Atlantic*, 8 December 2017, https://www. theatlantic.com/membership/archive/2017/12/the-irresistible-effectiveness-of-wedge-politics/547946

59 Jones, 'A Unity Ticket to Challenge the Integrity Vacuum in Canberra'.

60 C McGowan, *Cathy Goes to Canberra*, Monash University Press, Melbourne, 2020, p. 59.

61 Quoted in L Spencer, 'Uncommon Victories: Lessons from Warringah and Indi', *Australia Remade*, https://www. australiaremade.org/blog/uncommonvictories

62 Tony Windsor interview with Barrie Cassidy, *Insiders*, ABC, 30 June 2013.

63 Zoe Daniel campaign launch speech, Sandringham, Melbourne, 27 November 2021.

64 B Evans, 'The Battle for Hume Heats up', *Inside Story*, 19 November 2021, https://insidestory.org.au/the-battle-for-hume-heats-up

65 Tim Wilson letter to Goldstein constituents, November 2021.

66 J Clifford and K Fuller, 'Voices of Hume Candidate Penny Ackery to Take on Angus Taylor in 2022 Federal Election', *ABC News*, 14 November 2021, https://www.abc.net.au/news/2021-11-14/penny-ackery-to-take-on-angus-taylor-in-2022-federal-election/100618234

67 Allegra Spender campaign launch speech, Paddington, Sydney, 27 November 2021.

68 Ludlum, *Full Circle*, p. 254.

69 A Davies, 'Backed by Climate 200's $3.6m War Chest, Independent Candidates Circle Coalition Seats', *The Guardian*, 13 November 2021, https://www.theguardian.com/ australia-news/2021/nov/13/backed-by-climate-200s-2m-war- chest-independent-challengers-circle-coalition-seats

70 J Brett, *Doing Politics: Writings on Public Life*, Text Publishing, Melbourne, 2021, p. 17.

71 N Evershed, 'Was Julia Gillard the Most Productive Prime Minister in Australia's History?', *The Guardian*, 28 June 2013, https://www.theguardian.com/news/datablog/2013/jun/28/ australia-productive-prime-minister

72 A Applebaum, *Twilight of Democracy: The Failure of Politics and the Parting of Friends*, Penguin Random House, London, 2020, p. 189.